THE POCKET
INTERPRETER
CHINESE

FOREIGN LANGUAGES PRESS

First Edition 1988
Sixth Printing 2006

Edited by: Zeng Huijie

Home Page:
http://www.flp.com.cn
E-mail Addresses:
info@flp.com.cn
sales@flp.com.cn

ISBN 7-119-00557-X

Published by Foreign Languages Press
24 Baiwanzhuang Road, Beijing 100037, China

Distributed by China International Book Trading Corporation
35 Chegongzhuang Xilu, Beijing 100044, China
P.O.Box 399, Beijing, China

Printed in the People's Republic of China

Contents

Introduction

Pronunciation Guide

SIDEBARS

Introduction

Going to China is a dream come true for many West-
erners. In recent years, the opportunities for business, vacation, and educational trips have increased
rapidly. Without some knowledge of the Chinese language, however, you will find yourself either confined
to hotels and offices where English is spoken or totally
dependent on the services of an interpreter. To help
you have some independence while in China, *The
Pocket Interpreter*: *Chinese* provides the sentence
patterns you will most often need and the vocabulary
with which you can create new sentences. In addi-
tion, each chapter includes brief information which
will help you better understand the Chinese people,
their society, and their culture.

The design of this book is to offer basic sentences
upon which other sentences can be patterned, rather
than attempt to provide specific phrases for every situation the China traveler could possibly encounter.
You can use this book effectively by mastering the
basic patterns, such as "*... zài năr*? " (Where

is...?) and "*Yǒu méi yǒu...*?" (Do you have...?),
and referring to the dictionary for the specific words
you need to make the sentence you want. The twen-
ty-two sentence patterns introduced in Chapter One
recur often in the subsequent chapters. By recogniz-
ing the patterns each time they reappear, you will
soon be able to use them on your own.

In the patterns, the words for which substitutions
can be made have been bracketed in both the English
and Chinese pinyin versions. Thus you will know where
to replace a given word with one that is more suited to
your needs. For example, if the English sentence is
"Where is the (zoo)?" the corresponding Chinese
would be "(*Dòngwùyuán*) *zài nǎr*?" Seeing that
dòngwùyuán

is the equivalent of zoo, you could then look up another word in the dictionary, such as museum, and
substitute its Chinese equivalent, *bówùguǎn*, in the
given sentence. "Where is the museum?" would thus
be "*Bówùguǎn zài nǎr*?"

The Chinese words in this book have been spelled
according to the pinyin system, the officiall transliter-
ation of Putonghua used in the People's Republic of
China. Putonghua, also known as Mandarin, is the
national dialect of China. Based on a northern dialect, similar to that of Beijing, it is used in national
broadcasts and taught in public schools throughout
China. When among people of their own locality,

however, Chinese still speak their own local dialects, which vary greatly from region to region. In Guangzhou, for example, you will hear people around you speaking Cantonese, which bears almost no resemblance to Putonghua. Nevertheless, Putonghua is generally understood and you can use it wherever you go in China.

Since most Chinese do not read pinyin easily, the phrases here have also been given in Chinese characters, or *Hànzì*. The *Hànzì* used are the simplified characters of China, which are slightly different from the traditional characters used in Taiwan, Hong Kong, Singapore, and other places. People who know the traditional characters can usually figure out the simplified forms by context. If you have difficulty pronouncing a Chinese word or phrase, you can point to the accompanying *Hànzì* and ask the Chinese with whom you wish to communicate to read it.

Every Chinese written character represents a one-syllable word. Many Chinese words, however, are compounds composed of two or more characters which each contribute meaning to the total concept. For example, the word for movie is *diànyǐng*(电影), composed of the words *diàn* (electric) and *yǐng* (shadow). For ease of reading, the two syllables have been spelled together as one word in pinyin; in *Hànzì* they are two separate characters.

In Putonghua, each syllable is composed of an ini-

*tial sound, a final sound, and a tone. (**See charts, pp.**4-5)*The word **diàn**, for example, has the initial sound **d**, the final sound **ian**, and the downward fourth tone (ˋ). You will notice that some words in pinyin do not have tonal marks above them. This is because they are unstressed syllables which should be spoken quickly in a neutral tone.

A few words, such as **yī** (one), are not always marked with the same tone when they appear in different phrases. This is because the tone of some words depends on the tone of the word following it. **Yī**, for example, should only be spoken in the first tone when it stands alone or is followed by a pause; if the next word is a first-, second-, or third-tone word, **yī** should be read as **yì**; if the next word is a fourth-tone word, **yī** should be read as **yí**. Similarly **bù** (not) should be read as **bú** when the word following it is a fourth-tone word. For convenience, **yī** and **bù** have been marked in this book according to the tones in which they should be read within the phrase given, not as they are listed in the dictionary.

The tone, or inflection, of a Chinese word is just as important as its pronunciation. This aspect of speaking Chinese is the most difficult for English speakers to learn. In English, the tone of a word varies with the mood of the sentence; in Chinese, the tone stays the same whether the sentence is a question, exclamation, or matter-of-fact statement. Mood is indicated by stress on certain words, rather than inflection. To use the wrong tone in a Chinese word would be the equivalent of saying "cat" for "dog" in English.

The key to learning a new language is repetition. Begin by practicing a few simple phrases, such as *nǐhǎo* (hello) and *xièxie* (thank you), which you can use many times a day. Then build up to the useful phrases presented in Chapter One. To perfect your Putonghua, ask a Chinese friend to help you with your pronunciations and tones. Also, reinforce your grasp of the language by listening and looking. Be on the alert for the commonly heard phrases and often see signs presented at the end of each chapter. With these thoughts in mind, a positive outlook, and book in hand, *Yílùshùnfēng* (may good winds follow you)!

Pronunciation Guide

TONES

First Tone ▬ a relatively high, level tone, as when singing the note "la"

Second Tone ╱ a rising tone, as in "far" when asking, "Is it far?"

Third Tone ╲╱ a dipping tone, as when irritably saying, "So?"

Fourth Tone ╲ a downward tone, as when adamantly saying, "No!"

INITIAL SOUNDS

b, d, f, g, h	
j, k, l, m, n,	roughly the same as in English
p, s, t, w, y	
ch, sh	as in English, but curl the tongue up toward the roof of the mouth while pronouncing the "ch" or "sh" sound
c	ts as in cats
q	ch as in cheese
r	zhr, like in pleasure
x	sh as in banshee
z	ds as in cards
zh	dg as in fudge

FINAL SOUNDS

a	ah
ai	eye
an	ahn
ang	ahng
ao	ow
ar	are
e	uh
ei	eigh as in a sleigh
en	un as in run
eng	ung as in hung
er	cross between ar and er
i	ee, but after c, ch, r, s, sh, z, and zh it is silent
ia	ee-ah (quickly, as one syllable)
ian	ee-en (quickly)
iang	ee-ahng (quickly)
iao	ee-ow (quickly)
ie	ee-eh (quickly)
in	een as in seen
ing	ing as in ring
iong	ee-ōng (quickly)
iu	eo as in Leo
o	o as in or
ong	ōng
ou	oh
u	oo as in moo
ü	cross between oo and eew, as in French tu
ua	wa as in wash
uai	why
uan	wahn, as in wander
uang	wahng
ue	weh
ui	way
un	won
uo	wo as in wore

一 yī 1 Essentials

Méi bànfǎ.
Tough luck
(there's no other way).

How do you even begin to learn Chinese? When you arrive in China, you will find yourself suddenly the "foreigner." At first you may feel at a loss, not knowing what to say. Gradually, by learning a few essentials, you will find your new surroundings less formidable. The sentence patterns and phrases introduced here are the ones you will draw upon most often in your travels. Master these, and you'll be able to tackle China on your own.

ESSENTIALS

22 Sentence Patterns

Can I (enter)?	*Wǒ néng bù néng* (*jìnqu*)?
Can you (help me)?	*Nǐ néng bù néng* (*bāngmáng*)?
Do you have (postcards)?	*Yǒu* (*míngxìnpiàn*) *ma*?
How much does (this) cost?	(*Zhèige*) *yào duōshao qián*?
I am (American).	*Wǒ shì* (*Měiguó rén*)
I am not (a movie star).	*Wǒ bú shì* (*diànyǐng míngxīng*)
I have (two pieces of luggage).	*Wǒ yǒu* (*liǎng jiàn xíngli*).
I do not have (a map).	*Wǒ méi yǒu* (*dìtú*).
I lost my (passport).	*Wǒde* (*hùzhào*) *diū le*.
I need (to see a doctor).	*Wǒ yào* (*kànbìng*).
I do not need (a taxi).	*Wǒ bú yào* (*chūzū qìchē*).
I would like to (go to the zoo).	*Wǒ xiǎng* (*qù dòngwùyuán*).
I would not like to (rest).	*Wǒ bù xiǎng* (*xiūxi*)
I will stay in (Beijing) for [three days].	*Wǒ yào zài* (*Běijīng*) *dāi* [*sān tiān*].
Is there a (restaurant) nearby?	*Fùjìn yǒu* (*fànguǎn*) *ma*?
Please give me (a receipt).	*Qǐng gěi wǒ* (*fāpiào*).
Please help me (register).	*Qǐng bāng wǒ* (*dēngjì*).
This is my (shoulder bag).	*Zhè shì wǒde* (*bēibāo*).
This is not my (camera):	*Zhè bú shì wǒde* (*zhàoxiàngjī*).
When does (the bank) open?	(*Yínháng*) *shénme shíhou kāimén*?
Where can I find (coffee)?	*Nǎr yǒu* (*kāfēi*)?

2

我能不能进去?

你能不能帮忙?

有明信片吗?

这个要多少钱?

我是美国人。

我不是电影明星。

我有两件行李。

我没有地图。

我的护照丢了。

我要看病。

我不要出租汽车。

我想去动物园。

我不想休息

我要在北京呆三天。

附近有饭馆吗?

请给我发票。

请帮我登记。

这是我的背包。

这不是我的照相机。

银行什么时候开门?

哪儿有咖啡?

NO Verb conjugations

The easy part of learning Chinese is that there are no verb conjugations. I you, he, we, and they, all take the same verb form. For example:

I am   *wǒ shì*
You are   *Nǐ shì*
He is   *Tā shì*
we are   *wǒmen shì*
You are (pl)   *Nǐmen shì*
They are   *Tāmen shì*

The pronouns are also easy to remember. The plural forms are the singular forms plus the syllable *men*(们).

Where? There!

You will find that people from different regions in China prefer different words to express the same idea, and Putonghua incorporates these variations. For example, *nǎr* and *nǎli* both mean "where" and *nàr* and *nàli*, likewise, mean "there". People in the north tend to prefer the "r" sound, as in *nǎr*, whereas southemers prefer a crisper sound, as in *nǎli*.

Negatives

The negative form of most verbs in Chinese is formed by adding the syllable *bù*(不) before the verb, almost like the word"not" in English. For example.

I know.   *wǒ zhīdao.*
I don't know.   *wǒ bù zhīdao.*

However, with the verb *yǒu* (to have), the negative is formed with the syllable *méi*(没).

continued

3

ESSENTIALS

Where is (the post office)?	(Yóujú) zài nǎr?

Self-introduction

Hello.	Nǐhǎo.
My name is (John Smith).	Wǒ jiào (John Smith).
My last name is (Smith).	Wǒ xìng (Smith).
We're a group of five.	Wǒmen gòng yǒu (wǔ) gè rén.
We're with (XYZ Company).	Wǒmen shì (XYZ Gōngsī) de.

Courtesies

May I have your last name, Please?	Nín guì xìng?
Thank you.	Xièxie.
You're welcome.	Bú kèqi
Sorry.	Duìbuqǐ
I'm so sorry.	Zhēn duìbuqǐ.
It's nothing.	méi guānxi.
Excuse me(may I trouble you)...	Máfán nǐ...
Excuse me (may I ask)...	Qǐng wèn...
Excuse me (sorry).	Duìbuqǐ.
Excuse me (make way, hate to disturb you)...	Láojià...
I'm leaving now. Bye!	Wǒ zǒu le. Zàijiàn!

Key phrases

What's this?	Zhè shì shénme?
Which one?	Něige?
This one.	Zhèige.

4

邮局在哪儿?

你好!

我叫 John Smith.

我姓 Smith.

我们共有五个人。

我们是 X Y Z 公司的。

您贵姓?

谢谢。

不客气。

对不起。

真对不起!

没关系。

麻烦你……。

请问……。

对不起

劳驾……。

我走了,再见!

这是什么?

哪个?

这个。

He has money.	*Tā yǒu qián.*
He doesn't have money.	*Tā **méi** yǒu qián.*

Questions

Questions are formed in Chinese by adding the syllable ***ma***(吗) at the end of a statement or by inserting the negative form of a verb or modifier immediately after that verb or modifier. For example:

He is your friend.
Tā shì nǐde péngyǒu.
Is he your friend?
*Tā shì nǐde péngyǒu **ma***?
Is he (or is he not) your friend?
*Tā shì **bú shì** nǐde péngyǒu*?

Measure words

One of the most difficult skills in Chinese is the use of measure words. Every noun has a specific measure word that is used to count or refer to it, just like "gaggle" refers to geese and "pride" refers to lions in English.

The generic measure word in Chinese is ***gè*** (个) which can refer to almost anything. However, use of specific measure words is more proper. The proper measure word for books, for example, is ***běn*** (tome or edition). Whenever books are mentioned, ***běn*** precedes ***shū*** (book):

one book	*yì **běn** shū*
this book	*zhèi **běn** shū*
five book	*wǔ **běn** shū*
which book?	*něi **běn** shū*?

For a list of common measure words, refer to Appendix B on page 199.

ESSENTIALS

That one	*Nèige*.
Right.	*Duì*
Wrong.	*Bú duì*
Enough.	*Gòu le*.
Just right.	*Zhèng hǎo*.
How far?	*Duōyuǎn?*
How long(duration)?	*Duōjiǔ?*
How much?	*Duōshao?*
What time is it?	*Xiànzài jǐdiǎn le?*

Bridging the Gap

I don't understand.	*Wǒ bù míngbái*.
Please speak more slowly.	*Qǐng shuō de màn yìdiǎn*
Please point to it.	*Qǐng zhǐ gěi wǒ kàn*.
Will you please repeat that?	*Qǐng chóng fù yí biàn*.
Could you write it down?	*Nǐ néng xiě xià lai ma?*
How do you pronounce this?	*Zhèige zěnme niàn?*
What does this mean?	*Zhè shì shénme yìsi?*

Emergencies

Help!	*Jiù mìng!*
Call the police.	*Kuài jiào jǐngchá*.
Get a doctor.	*Kuài jiào yīshēng lái*.
There's a fire.	*Nà biān qǐhuǒ le*.
There's been an accident.	*Nà biān chūshì le*.

那个。
对。
不对。
够了。
正好。
多远?
多久?
多少?
现在几点了?

我不明白。
请说得慢一点。
请指给我看。
请重复一遍。
你能写下来吗?
这个怎么念?
这是什么意思?

救命!
快叫警察。
快叫医生来。
那边起火了。
那边出事了。

Past Tense

The past tense of a verb in Chinese is mabe by adding the syllable *le* (了) immediately after the verb or at the very end of the sentence, For example:

I'm going.   *Wǒ qù*
I went.   *Wǒ qù le*。
I went shopping   *Wǒ qù mǎi dōngxi le*.

Zheige or zhege?

You might wonder why there is an inconsistency in the pronunciation, and pinyin spelling, of *zhè* (这), meaning "this"; *nà* (那), meaning "that"; and *nǎ* (哪), meaning "which." When the word following these indicators is a measure word, then *zhè* is often pronounced *zhèi*; *nà* is pronounced *nèi* or *nè*; and *nǎ* is pronounced *něi*. For example:

this one   *zhège, zhèige*
that one   *nàge, nèige, nège*
which one?   *nǎge? něige?*

What You'll Hear

bù hǎo	no good
bù xíng	not okay; doesn't work
děng yì děng	wait a while
hǎo	good
kě yǐ	can be done
Méi bànfǎ.	There's no solution.
Méi yǒu	There isn't any.
Qǐng jìn	Please come in.
Xíng	okay
Wèi!	Hello. Hey!

Signs

rùkǒu
Entrance

chūkǒu
Exit

nán cèsuǒ
Men's Toilets

nǚ cèsuǒ
Women's Toilets

gōngyòng diànhuà
Public Telephone

Travel 2 二 èr

Yí lù shùnfēng!
Bon voyage
(good winds all the way)!

Traveling through China is fun. Making your own
arrangements for travel, or being delayed in an airport
or train station for several hours, however, is another
story! At those times when good communication is so
necessary, the phrases here can help.

TRAVEL

Asking for information

Is there (travel service office) nearby?	*Fùjìn yǒu (lǚxíng shè) ma?*
Where is the (long-distance bus station)?	*(Chángtú qìchē zhàn) zài nǎr?*
I'm looking for a (CITS) representative.	*Wǒ xiàng zhǎo (Guó Lǚ) de rén.*
Which direction is the (train station)?	*Qù (huǒchē zhàn) wǎng nǎge fāng xiàng zǒu?*
Where am I supposed to go?	*wǒ gāi wǎng nǎli zǒu?*

Identification

This is my (passport).	*Zhè shì wǒde (hùzhào).*
I'm traveling with my (wife or husband).	*Wǒ shì hé wǒ (àirén) yìqǐ lái de*
We're all together.	*Wǒmen dōu shì yìqǐ lái de.*
I've come to (sightsee).	*Wǒ shì lái (guānguāng) de.*
I am going to (Shanghai).	*Wǒ yào qù (Shànghǎi).*
I will stay there (eight) days.	*Wǒ yào zài nàli dāi (bā tiān).*

Booking a Ticket

I'd like to buy (two) ticket to [xi'an].	*Wǒ yào mǎi (liǎng) zhāng qù [xī'ān] de piào.*
I'd like a (round-trip) ticket.	*Wǒ yào mǎi yì zhāng (láihuí) piào.*
I'd like to leave on the (9th) and return on the [17th].	*Wǒ (jiǔ hào) líkāi, [shíqīhào] huílai.*
How much is a (one-way) ticket to [Tianjin]?	*Qù [Tiānjīn] de (dānchéng) piào duōshao qián?*
Are there (soft-sleeper) tickets available?	*Hái yǒu (ruǎnwò) piào ma?*

附近有旅行社吗？

长途汽车站在哪
儿？

我想找国旅的人。

去火车站往哪个
方向走？

我该往哪里走？

这是我的护照。

我是和我爱人一
起来的。

我们都是一起来的。

我是来观光的。

我要去上海。

我要在那里呆八天。

我要买两张去西
安的票。

我要买一张来回
票。

我九号离开，十七
号回来。

去天津的单程票
多少钱？

还有软卧票吗？

International Airlines

　　Many international airlines now land
in either Shanghai or Beijing. When
booking a flight, you may need to know
the Chinese name for your chosen air-
line, Here are the names and codes of
some airlines with service to China.

Air France AF	Fǎguó Hángkōng Gōngsi 法国航空公司
British Airways BA	Yīngguó Hángkōng Gōngsi 英国航空公司
Canadian Airlines Int'l CP	jiānádà Guójì Hángkōng Gōngsī 加拿大国际航空公司
Japan Air Lines JL	Rìběn Hángkōng Gōngsi 日本航空公司
Lufthansa LH	Déguó Hànshā Hángkōng Gōngsi 德国汉莎航空公司
Philippine Air Lines PR	Fēilǜbīn Hángkōng Gōngsi 菲律宾航空公司
Singapore Airlines SQ	Xīnjiāpō Hángkōng Gōngsi 新加坡航空公司
Swiss Air SR	Ruìshì Hángkōng Gōngsi 瑞士航空公司
Thai Airways Int'l TG	Tàiguó Guójì Hángkōng Gōngsi 泰国国际航空公司
United Airlines UA	Měiguó Liánhé Hángkōng Gōngsi 美国联合航空公司

TRAVEL

Is there a discount for (children)?	(*xiǎoháir*) piào piányi diǎn *ma*?
How many stopovers are there enroute?	*Lùshàng yào tíng jǐ zhàn?*
When is the next (express train)?	*Xià cì* (*tèkuài*) *shì shénme shíjiān de?*
When is the next (ship) to [Wuhan]?	*Qù* (*wǔhàn*) *de xià bān* (*chuán*) *shì shénme shíjiān de?*
Is there a (morning) train?	*Yǒu* (*zǎochén*) *de huǒchē ma?*
Is there an (evening) flight?	*Yǒu* (*wǎnshang*) *de hángbān ma?*
When is the last bus to (Chengde)?	*Qù* (*Chéngdé*) *de zuìhòu yí tàng qìchē shì shénme shíjiān?*
How long does it take by (train)?	*Zuò huǒchē yào duō jiǔ?*
What time should I arrive at the (airport)?	*Wǒ gāi shénme shíhou dào* (*jīchǎng*)?

Watiting to Board

Where shall I go to (check in)?	*Wǒ yīnggāi dào nǎr qù* (*bàn shǒuxù*)?
When will flight no. (123) take off?	(*Yībǎièrshísān*) *cì hángbān shénme shíhou qǐfēi?*
When will train no. (45) depart?	(*Sìshíwǔ*) *cì huǒchē shénme shíhou kāi?*
When will the bus to (Beidaihe) leave?	*Qù* (*Běidàihé*) *de qìchē shénme shíhou kāi?*
When will the train to (Luoyang) leave?	*Qù* (*Luòyáng*) *de huǒchē shénme shíhou kāi?*

小孩票便宜点吗？

路上要停几站？

下次特快是什么
时间的？

去武汉的下班船
是什么时间的？

有早晨的火车吗？

有晚上的航班吗？

去承德的最后一趟
汽车是什么时间？

坐火车要多久？

我该什么时候到
机场？

我应该到哪儿去
办手续？

123 次航班什么时
候起飞？

45 次火车什么时
候开？

去北戴河的汽车
什么时候开？

去洛阳的火车什
么时候开？

What Kind of Plane Is This?

To meet the growing demands of visitors and business people who travel by air, the Civil Aviation Administration of China（CAAC）has been importing foreign aircraft as well as establishing joint ventures with foreign aircraft manufacturers. In the 1950s and 1960s, China's domestic routes were flown mainly by Soviet-made airplanes. Today, many of the planes are American or Western European models. Yor may ask the flight attendant, *Wǒmen zuò de fēijī shì shénme xínghào de?* (What model of plane are we on?) and use the list below for reference.

Aerospace (British)	*Yǔháng Gōngsī* 宇航公司
Airbus (European)	*Kōngzhōng kèchē* 空中客车
Antonow (Russia)	*Ān* 安
Boeing (USA)	*Bōyīn* 波音
Ilyushin (Russia)	*Yī'ěr* 伊尔
McDonnell Douglas (USA)	*Màikètángnà Dàogélāsi* 麦克唐纳·道格拉斯
Shorts 360 (European)	*Xiāotè Sānliùlíng* 肖特三六〇
Trident (British)	*Sānchàjǐ* 三叉戟

TRAVEL

Is there any news about flight no. (789)?	*(Qībǎi bāshí jiǔ) cì hángbān yǒu xiāoxi ma?*
How much longer do we have to wait?	*Wǒmen háiyào děng duōjiǔ?*
Will I make the connecting fight?	*Wǒ néng gǎnshàng xiánjiē hángbān ma?*
Is there a (telephone) nearby?	*Fùjìn yǒu (diànhuà) ma?*
Please help me reroute my ticket.	*Qǐng bāng wǒ gǎi yíxià hángbān.*

All Aboard

Can you help me (store) this?	*Nǐ néng bāng wǒ bǎ zhège (cún qǐlai) ma?*
When will we arrive at (Lhasa)?	*Wǒmen shénme shíhou néng dào (Lāsà)?*
How is the weather in (Chengdu)?	*(Chéngdū) de tiānqì zěnmeyàng?*
This (seat belt) is broken.	*Zhège (ānquándài) huài le.*
Can you turn on the (air-conditioning)?	*Qǐng bǎ (kōngtiáo) dǎkāi, hǎo ma?*
Where are we now?	*Wǒmen xiànzài dào nǎli le?*
What is that outside?	*Wàimiàn nàge shì shénme?*
What is the next station?	*Xià zhàn shì nǎli?*
What model of (plane) is this?	*Zhège (fēijī) shì shénme xínghào?*
Will you please let me know when we're almost at (Suzhou)?	*Kuài dào (Sūzhōu) de shíhòu qǐng tōngzhī wǒ yíxià.*
How long will we stop here?	*Wǒmen yào zài zhèli tíng duōjiǔ?*

789 次航班有消息
吗？

我们还要等多久？

我能赶上衔接航
班吗？

附近有电话吗？

请帮我改一下航
班。

你能帮我把这个
存起来吗？

我们什么时候能
到拉萨？

成都的天气怎么
样？

这个安全带坏了。

请把空调打开好
吗？

我们现在到哪里了？

外面那个是什么？

下站是哪里？

这个飞机是什么
型号？

快到苏州的时候
请通知我一下。

我们要在这里停
多久？

Tuplev (Russia)	*Tú* 图
Twin Otter (USA)	*Shuāngshuǐtǎ* 双水獭
Yun (PRC)	*Yùn* 运

Good, Better, Best

Comparatives and superlatives in Chinese are formed by adding an extra word or two to the original modifier. The pattern is always the same. For example:

good	*hǎo*
better	*hǎo yìdiǎn* (*yìxiē*)
even better	*gèng hǎo*
best	*zuìhǎo*
fast	*kuài*
faster	*kuài yìdiǎn* (*yìxiē*)
even faster	*gèng kuài*
fastest	*zuìkuài*

The Chinese culture being a polite one, the first way of suggesting something more than the original is by adding *yìdiǎn* (a little) or *yìxiē* (some) after the modifier, thus implying something somewhat better but not a lot better. A stronger version of the comparative is formed by inserting *gèng* (even) before the modifier. The superlative is formed by inserting the word *zuì* (most)

The Best in Life

Traditionally Chinese have regarded luck, wealth, longevity, and happiness as the four blessings in life. You will find these four characters appearing on many

TRAVEL

What time do we have to be back on board?

Wǒmen jǐdiǎn bìxū huílai?

Baggage Claim

Where is the (baggage claim area)?

(Xíngli fáng) zài nǎr?

I can't find my (suitcase).

Wǒde (xiāngzi) zhǎo bú dào le.

This is my (baggage claim tag).

zhè shì wǒde (xíngli pái).

Are there any (carts)?

Yǒu (xiǎo tuīchē) ma?

Can someone help me (carry my bags)?

Yǒu rén néng bāng wǒ (tí yíxià xíngli) ma?

Where is the (exit)?

(Chūkǒu) zài nǎr?

Customs

This is mine.

Zhè shì wǒde.

This is not mine.

Zhè bú shì wǒde.

These are my (personal effects).

Zhè shì wǒde (sīrén wùpǐn).

I am not carrying any (precious jewelry).

Wǒ méi dài rènhé (zhūbǎo).

This is a (reproduction).

Zhè shì (fùzhìpǐn).

I'm not familiar with (these regulations).

Wǒ bú tài shúxī (zhèxiē guīdìng).

It's in my (wife's) suitcase.

Zài wǒ (qīzi de) xiāngzi lǐ.

I lost it.

Diū le.

I gave it away.

Sòng rén le.

This is my (first) trip to China this year.

Zhè shì wǒ jīnnián (dì yī) cì lái Zhōngguó.

How much is the duty?

Shuìkuǎn duōshao?

我们几点必须回来？

行李房在哪儿？

我的箱子找不到了。

这是我的行李牌。

有小推车吗？

有人能帮我提一下行李吗？

出口在哪儿？

这是我的。

这不是我的。

这是我的私人物品。

我没带任何珠宝。

这是复制品。

我不太熟悉这些规定。

在我妻子的箱子里。

丢了。

送人了。

这是我今年第一次来中国。

税款多少？

decorative objects, either singly or all four together.

福 *fú* (luck)

禄 *lù* (wealth)

壽 *shòu* (longevity)

喜 *xǐ* (happiness)

Good-byes

There are many ways to say good-bye in Chinese. Here are some of the most often used ones.

Huítóu jiàn.	See you soon.
Míngtiān jiàn.	See you tomorrow.
Xià cì jiàn.	See you next time.
Yíhuìr jiàn.	See you later.
Zàijiàn.	See you again.

What you'll Hear

Dào le.	We've arrived.
Gèwèi lǚkè, qǐng zhùyì...	Attention travelers...
Nǐ qù nǎr?	Where are you going?
Qǐng náchū nǐde...	Please show your...
dēngjī pái	boarding pass
hǎiguān shēnbào dān	customs declaration
hùzhào	passport
qiānzhèng	visa
zhàoxiàngjī	camera
Shì nǐde ma?	Is this yours?

Signs

jīchǎng
Airport

hòuchēshì
**Waiting Room
(for trains, buses)**

kāiwǎng...
Leaving for...

fēiyǐnyòng shuǐ
Unpotable Water

jìnzhǐ xīyān
No Smoking

三 sān 3 Local Transport

Xiàma?
Getting off?

In China, local transportation is available in many forms. You can get around town by taxi, hired car, public bus, bicycle, or "bus no. **11**," which simply means walking ("**11**"representing two legs). In Beijing, Shanghai, Guangzhou you can also ride the subway, or *dìtiě*. The most important thing to learn is how to ask for directions, and then understanding the answer.

LOCAL TRANSPORT

Getting Set

I'd like a (local) map, please.
Qǐng gěi wǒ yì zhāng (běndì) dìtú.

Can I get some directions.
Néng wèn yíxià lù ma?

I'd like to go to (the Big Goose Pagoda).
Wǒ xiǎng qù (Dàyàn Tǎ).

What's the best way to get there?
Něi tiáo lù zuìjìn?

How far is it to (People's Park)?
Qù (Rénmín Gōngyuán) yǒu duōyuǎn?

Is it within walking distance?
Zǒu de dào ma?

How much should the fare be to (the airport)?
Qù (jīchǎng) yào duōshǎo qián?

Taking a Taxi

Where can I get a taxi?
Nǎr néng jiàodào chūzū qìchē?

Can you send a taxi?
Nǐmen néng pài liàng chūzūchē ma?

I'd like a cab to (the Exhibition Center).
Wǒ yào qù (zhǎnlǎn Zhōngxīn)

What's the fare per kilometer?
Yì gōnglǐ duōshao qián?

To (the Peace Hotel), please.
Qǐng kāi dào (Hépíng Fàndiàn).

Driver, can you take me to (this address)?
Sījī, nǐ néng bǎ wǒ sòng dào (zhège dìfāng) ma?

Do you know the way there?
Nǐ zhīdao zěnme zǒu ma?

Please stop a moment.
Qǐng tíng yíxià.

Please drive (faster).
Qǐng kāi (kuài yìdiǎn).

Make a right at the light.
Zài hónglǜdēng yòu zhuǎn

Which Way Is North?

After you ask someone on the street for directions, listen for these key words in their answer:

北	*běi*	north
东	*dōng*	east
南	*nán*	south
西	*xī*	west
右	*yòu*	right
左	*zuǒ*	left
后	*hòu*	back
前	*qián*	front

Some common expressions used for giving directions are:

guò...	past (across)...
hóng lǜ dēng	the stoplight
mǎ lù	the road
wǎng...guǎi	turn toward...
wǎng...zǒu	walk toward...
yìzhí zǒu	go straight on
zài...biān	on the ...side
zài...miàn	facing the...
zǒu cuò le	wrong way

Taxi Fares

In China, every legitimate taxi is metered. Most taxis belong to state-owned taxi companies, which operate either as independent car services or in connection with travel agencies, hotels, or restaurants. Recently there has been a rise of gypsy cabs on the streets—be careful of them. When you enter a cab, make sure the driver turns on the meter. If he doesn't, say *Qǐng dǎkāi jìjiàqì* (please turn on the meter). If he still

请给我一张本地地图。

能问一下路吗？

我想去大雁塔。

哪条路最近？

去人民公园有多远？

走得到吗？

去机场要多少钱？

哪儿能叫到出租汽车？

你们能派辆出租车吗？

我要去展览中心。

一公里多少钱？

请开到和平饭店。

司机，你能把我送到这个地方吗？

你知道怎么走吗？

请停一下。

请开快一点。

在红绿灯右转。

LOCAL TRANSPORT

Can you wait for me?	*Néng děng wǒ yíxià ma?*
I'll be back in (20) minutes.	*Wǒ (èrshí) fēnzhōng yǐhòu huílai.*
Then I'd like to return to (the hotel).	*Ránhòu wǒ jiù huí (fàndiàn).*
This is the wrong way.	*Zǒu cuò lù le.*
Don't try to trick me.	*Bié piàn wǒ.*

Hiring a Car

I'd like to hire (a car).	*Wǒ yào bāo (yí liàng chē).*
What is the rate per (day)?	*Měi (tiān) duōshao zūjīn?*
Can I hire a car for (half a day)?	*Bāo (bàntiān) chē xíng ma?*
I'd like to rent a car one way.	*Wǒ xiǎng zū dānchéng chē*
After how many (Kilometers) will there be an extra charge?	*Chāoguò duōshao (gōnglǐ) yào lìngwài jiā qián?*
How do you charge for extra (mileage)?	*Chāoguò de (lǐchéng) zěnme shōufèi?*
Do you have a car available (now)?	*(Xiànzài) yǒu chē ma?*
I'd like to hire a car for (two) days beginning [the day after tommorow].	*Wǒ xiǎng cóng [hòutiān] qǐ bāo (liǎng) tiān chē.*
I'll come for the car at (8:00 in the morning).	*(Zǎochén bā diǎn) wǒ yào yòng chē.*
Buckle up!	*Qǐng jì shàng ānquán dài.*
Fill'er up!	*Jiā mǎn yóu!*
I have a flat tire.	*Wǒ de lúntāi méi qì le.*
My car broke down on the freeway.	*Wǒ de chē zài gāosù gōnglù shàng pāo máo le.*

能等我一下吗?

我二十分钟以后回来。

然后我就回饭店。

走错路了。

别骗我。

我要包一辆车。

每天多少租金。

包半天车行吗?

我想租单程车

超过多少公里要另外加钱?

超过的里程怎么收费?

现在有车吗?

我想从后天起包两天车。

早晨八点我要用车。

请系上安全带。

加满油!

我的轮胎没气了。

我的车在高速公路上抛锚了。

refuses to turn on the meter. the best you can do is strike a hard bargain for the fare to your destination.

Ten year ago, taxis were rare in Beijing, but nowadays you can see yellow or red cabs full of the street. They are cheap and convenient. There are normally three types of taxis in the street, with different fares. The ones larger, more comfortable ones, like Volkswagen or similar car, charge 2 yuan per kilometre, and the fare for smaller or older cars, called by locals "Xiali" is 1.20 yuan per kilometre. A new type of taxi, called by the locals "Fukang", charge 1.60 yuan per kilometre.

Bus Numbers

Buses in China are identified by their route number, so instead of saying *hào* (number) when referring to a bus, the Chinese say *lù* (route). Thus, bus no. 52 would be *wǔshí èr lù chē*.

Riding Public Buses

Public buses are the chief means of local transportation for Chinese urban residents, with fares costing from 1 yuan to 2 yuan depending on the distance traveled. After boarding a bus, you must make your way, if your can, to the nearest bus conductor who will be seated at a booth near one of the doors. Large buses will have more than one conductor. Tell the conductor how many tickets you want and to what destination; for example, *liǎng zhāng*, *Tiān'ān mén* (two tickets, Tian'an men). He or she will tell you theprice, such as 2 yuan , and give you a

LOCAL TRANSPORT

Going by Bus

Which bus should I take to get to (the Summer Palace)?
Qù (yíhéyuán) zuò něi lù chē?

Where is the nearest bus stop?
Zuìjìn de gōnggòng qìchē zhàn zài nǎr?

How many stops to (the zoo)?
Qù (dòngwùyuán) yǒu jǐ zhàn?

Does this bus go to the Beijing Library)?
zhè tàng chē qù (Běijīng Túshūguǎn) ma?

(One) ticket to [Wangfujing].
(Yì) Zhāng, (Wángfǔjǐng)

Please tell me when to get off.
Dào zhàn qǐng jiào wǒ yíxià.

Where can I transfer to bus no. (302)?
Zài nǎr néng dǎo (sān líng èr) lù chē?

Where is the bus stop for bus no. (41)?
(Sìshí yī) lù chēzhàn zài nǎr?

I came by the city streets.
Wǒ shì zǒu shìqū dàolù lái de.

I was tied up in traffic.
Wǒ yù dào sāi chē.

Riding the Subway

Is this a subway (entrance)?
Zhè shì dìtiě de (rùkǒu) ma?

Does this subway go to (Chongwenmen)?
Zhè tàng dìtiě qù (Chóngwénmén) ma?

Where should I wait for the subway to (Beijing Railway Staion)?
Qù (Běijīng Zhàn) zài nǎr děng chē?

What is the next stop?
Xià zhàn shì nǎr?

Make way, we want to get off.
Qǐng ràng yíxià, wǒmen yào xià chē.

去颐和园坐哪路车?

最近的公共汽车站在哪儿?

去动物园有几站?

这趟车去北京图书馆吗?

一张,王府井。

到站请叫我一下。

在哪儿能倒 302 路车?

41 路车站在哪儿?

我是走市区道路来的。

我遇到塞车。

这是地铁的入口吗?

这趟地铁去崇文门吗?

去北京站在哪儿等车?

下站是哪儿?

请让一下,我们要下车。

ticket stub. Keep the stub in case you need to show it later. If you notice that many Chinese do not buy tickets, it's probably because they have monthly passes, known as *yuè piào*.

When you have almost reached your stop, be sure to make your way to the door. On crowded buses it's easy to get packed in the middle of the bus and not be able to get off before the doors close and the bus moves on.

Bus Stops

Bus stops are marked by signposts along the road, or sometimes by small signs affixed to electricity poles or tree trunks. If the road is wide and an island separates it from the bicycle path, the bus stop will be on the island. The bus sign will show the route number, the name of the immediate stop, the destination toward which the bus is traveling, and the times of the first run and last run. A chart showing all the stops along the route is often included, with the immediate stop indicated by a box, an arrow, or underlining. Sometimes the sign also gives advance notice of the next stop, so be careful not to mix that up with the name of the current stop.

Some Chinese characters you will need to recognize are:

公共汽车	public bus
本站	this stop
下站	next stop
头班车	first run
首班车	first run
末班车	last run
夜班车	night bus

LOCAL TRANSPORT

On Foot

I'm trying to find (Elephant Trunk Hill).	*Wǒ zài zhǎo (xiàngbí shān).*
Can you direct me there?	*Nǐ néng gàosù wǒ zěnme zǒu ma?*
Does this lane lead to (the main street)?	*Zhè tiáo xiǎoxiàng tōngxiàng (dàjiē) ma?*
Excuse me, could you tell me where the (CAAC office) is?	*Láojià, nǐ néng gàosù wǒ (Zhōngguó Mínháng bànshìchù) zài nǎr ma?*
Is this (Chang'an Avenue)?	*Zhè shì (Cháng'ān Jiē) ma?*
Is this way (north)?	*Zhè shì (běi) miàn ma?*
I'm lost.	*Wǒ mílù le.*
Where am I?	*Wǒ xiànzài zài nǎr?*

Renting a Bike

I'd like to rent a bicycle.	*Wǒ xiǎng zū yī liàng zìxíngchē.*
How much is the rental for one (hour)?	*Yì (xiǎo shí) de zūjīn shì duōshao?*
How much is (the deposit)?	*(Yājīn) duōshao?*
I'd like that (blue) one.	*Wǒ yào nà liàng (lán) de.*
I'll bring it back around (4:00 in the afternoon).	*(Xiàwǔ sì diǎn) zuǒyòu wǒ lái huán chē.*
I've finished riding.	*Wǒ bú yòng chē le.*
How much do I owe?	*Duōshao qián?*
My (passport), please.	*Qǐng bǎ (hùzhào) huán wǒ.*

我在找象鼻山。

你能告诉我怎么走吗？

这条小巷通向大街吗？

劳驾，你能告诉我中国民航办事处在哪儿吗？

这是长安街吗？

这是北面吗？

我迷路了。

我现在在哪儿？

我想租一辆自行车。

一小时的租金是多少？

押金多少？

我要那辆蓝的

下午四点左右我来还车。

我不用车了。

多少钱？

请把护照还我。

Bicycle

The bicycle is the most popular means of transport in China. Nearly everybody has one. A great mass of people in city go to work by bike. It is a feast for eyes if you get up early in the morning and watch the great masses of bicycle streaming down the street. Of course, you can hire a bike at your hotel and riding around the streets is great fun, especially if you are going to visit the hutongs. But you have to be careful, especially at junctions and traffic, lights. Traffic in China is sometimes chaotic and rules about right of way and turning right at traffic lights may be different from your own country, so it is potentially confusing and dangerous, so take care.

What You'll Hear

dǎo chē	transfer buses
Dào nǎr?	Where to?
dǎ kāi piào	show your ticket
huàn chē	transfer buses
Kàn chē!	Watch out (for the bike or car)!
kuài chē	express
mǎi piào	buy a ticket
Xià ma?	Are you getting off?
Xiān xià,	Let people off first,
hòu shàng.	then get on.
Zhàn zhù.	Halt.

Signs

chūzūqìchē zhàn
Taxi Stand

zìxíngchē xiūlǐbù
Bicycle Repair Shop

(tíng)
No Parking

chū rù qǐng xià chē
Please Get off Your Bike at the Gate

shìgù duōfā dìduàn
Site of Frequent Accidents

四 sì 4 Hotel

Hotels have come a long way in China, especially since
the early **1980**s when Western tourists began arriving
in big waves. Whereas a "first-class hotel" used to
mean a **1950**s-style boardinghouse with simple
furniture, clean bedding, and keys hung on a pegboard,
these days it means a five-star hotel where you can find
everything from telex machines to a health club and
disco. The service people at the main desk usually
know enough English to handle common requests, but
the upstairs floor attendants may barely know any.

HOTEL

Checking In

I have already booked (one) room for [two] nights.

Wǒ yǐjīng yùdìng le (yí) gè fángjiān zhù [liǎng] gè wǎnshang.

Do you have a (single room) available?

Yǒu (dān jiān) ma?

How much is a (twin room) per night?

(Shuāngrén fángjiān) duōshao qián?

What is your lowest rate for a room?

(Zuìpiányi) de fángjiān shì duōshao qián?

I would like to stay (three) nights.

Wǒ xiǎng zhù (sān) tiān.

I would like (two) rooms next to each other.

Wǒ yào (liǎng) gè jǐnāizhe de fángjiān.

I would like a room facing the (garden).

Wǒ yào yì jiān chuānghu duìzhe (huāyuán) de fángjiān.

Does this room have a good (view)?

Zhège fángjiān (chuāngwài de fēngjǐng) hǎo ma?

I prefer a room on a (lower) floor.

Wǒ xiǎng yào (dǐ) céng de fángjiān.

Can an extra cot be brought in?

Néng zài jiā yì zhāng chuáng ma?

Do you give a discount to (foreign students)?

Duì (liúxuéshēng) yǒu méi yǒu yōuhuì?

Will I be able to pay by (credit card)?

Wǒ néng yòng (xìnyòngkǎ) fùkuǎn ma?

Checking Out

Please make up my bill.

Qǐng bāng wǒ jiézhàng.

My room number is (3024).

Wǒ zhù (sān líng èr sì) fángjiān.

我已经预定了一个房间，住两个晚上。

有单间吗？

双人房间多少钱？

最便宜的房间是多少钱？

我想住三天。

我要两个紧挨着的房间。

我要一间窗户对着花园的房间。

这个房间窗外的风景好吗？

我想要底层的房间。

能再加一张床吗？

对留学生有没有优惠？

我能用信用卡付款吗？

请帮我结帐。

我住 3024 房间。

Local Hostels

For those of you who are traveling on a shoestring, you might choose to stay at a *lǚguǎn* (small hotel), *lǚshè* (inn), or *sùshè* (dorm or hostel). The prices there are cheap, the most you'll pay being 60 yuan for a single room to 20 yuan for a room shared with three other people. The accommodations are spartan – a cot and a TV, often black and white, no closets, and a bathroom down the hallway. Remember also that running hot water is a luxury in China, so most small establishments will not have it. When hot water is provided, the hours are usually restricted.

To request a bed in a shared room, use the phrase *Hái yǒu chuáng wèi ma*? (Is there a berth available?)

Chinese Horoscope

The Chinese "horoscope" is represented by twelve animals, with one animal governing each year in a twelve-year cycle. Each animal represents one of the Twelve Earthly Branches in Chinese astrology.

Traditionally, Chinese have kept track of each other's ages by remembering what animal sign a person belongs to. For example, someone might forget how old his sister is but remember "Oh, she was born in the year of the tiger..." and figure it out from there. If you want to ask someone's age indirectly, say *Nì shǔ shénme*? (what do you belong to?) the twelve animals and their corresponding years in this century are listed below.

HOTEL

There seems to be a mistake here.	*Zhèli hǎoxiàng yǒu diǎn bú duì.*
I've paid already.	*Wǒ yǐjīng fù guò kuǎn le.*
When is check-out time?	*Shénme shíhou tuì fáng?*
I'll be leaving tomorrow morning at (7:30).	*Wǒ míngtiān zǎochén (qī diǎn bàn) zǒu.*
Where shall I leave the key?	*Yàoshi liú zài nǎr?*
Put it on my hotel bill, please.	*Qǐng suàn zài wǒde zhùsùfèi li.*

Service Inquiries

When will my (suitcases) be brought up?	*Wǒde (xíngli) shénme shíhou néng sòng shàng lái?*
Can it be brought to my room?	*Néng sòng dào wǒde fángjiān ma?*
Where shall I pick up (the keys)?	*Wǒ dào nǎr qù ná (yàoshi)?*
Do you have another (key) for my roommate?	*Wǒde tóngwū yě néng yǒu (yì bǎ yàoshi) ma?*
Have there been any messages for me?	*Yǒu rén gěi wǒ liúhuà ma?*
Where is the (elevator)?	*(Diàntī) zài nǎr?*
When is the (bar) open?	*(Jiǔbā) shénme shíhou kāimén?*
Do you have today's (China Daily)?	*Yǒu jīntiān de (Zhōngguó Rìbào) ma?*
Where can I find (the banquet manager)?	*Nǎr néng zhǎo dào (yànhuìtīng jīnglǐ)?*
Is there some place where I can send (a telex)?	*Nǎr néng fā (diànchuán)?*
Can you help me get my (watch) repaired?	*Nǐ néng bāng wǒ xiū yíxià (biǎo) ma?*

这里好像有点不对。

我已经付过款了。

什么时候退房？

我明天早晨七点半走。

钥匙留在哪儿？

请算在我的住宿费里。

我的行李什么时候能送上来？

能送到我的房间吗？

我到哪儿去拿钥匙？

我的同屋也能有一把钥匙吗？

有人给我留话吗？

电梯在哪儿？

酒吧什么时候开门？

有今天的《中国日报》吗？

哪儿能找到宴会厅经理？

哪儿能发电传？

你能帮我修一下表吗？

Rat *shǔ*	鼠	1912, 1924, 1936, 1948 1960, 1972, 1984, 1996
Ox *niú*	牛	1913, 1925, 1937, 1949 1961, 1973, 1985, 1997
Tiger *hǔ*	虎	1914, 1926, 1938, 1950 1962, 1974, 1986, 1998
Rabbit *tù*	兔	1915, 1927, 1939, 1951 1963, 1975, 1987, 1999
Dragon *lóng*	龙	1916, 1928, 1940, 1952 1964, 1976, 1988, 2000
Snake *shé*	蛇	1917, 1929, 1941, 1953 1965, 1977, 1989, 2001
Horse *mǎ*	马	1918, 1930, 1942, 1954 1966, 1978, 1990, 2002
Sheep *yáng*	羊	1907, 1919, 1931, 1943, 1955, 1967, 1979, 1991
Monkey *hóu*	猴	1908, 1920, 1932, 1944, 1956, 1968, 1980, 1992
Rooster *jī*	鸡	1909, 1921, 1933, 1945, 1957, 1969, 1981, 1993
Dog *gǒu*	狗	1910, 1922, 1934, 1946, 1958, 1970, 1982, 1994
Pig *zhū*	猪	1911, 1923, 1935, 1947, 1959, 1971, 1983, 1995

Long-distance Communications

Post offices in China are the centers for long-distance telephone calls and telegrams. If you are far away from a luxury hotel and need to call home, go to a main post office, However, be prepared to wait in line to place your call or telegram. International phone calls sometimes take over an hour for the connection to be made.

HOTEL

Please wake me up tomorrow at (6:00 am).	*Qǐng zài míngtiān (zǎochén liù diǎn) jiào xǐng wǒ.*

Problems in the Room

The (toilet) doesn't work.	*(Cèsuǒ) huài le.*
The (faucet) is leaking.	*(Lóngtóu) lòushuǐ.*
Please help me open the (windows).	*Qǐng bāng wǒ dǎkāi (chuānghu).*
The door doesn't lock.	*Zhèige mén suǒ bú shàng.*
How do you turn on the (heat)?	*Zěnme kāi (nuǎnqì)?*
How do you adjust this (digital clock)?	*Zhège (diànzǐbiǎo) zěnme tiáo?*
My room is too (noisy).	*Wǒde fángjiān tài (chǎo) le.*
I'd like to change to another room.	*Wǒ xiǎng huàn yí gè fángjiān.*

Housekeeping

I need (some towels).	*Wǒ xiǎng yào (jǐ tiáo máojīn).*
May I borrow an (iron)?	*Wǒ xiǎng jiè yí gè (yùn dǒu).*
Please bring (a thermos of boiled water).	*Qǐng ná (yì píng kāishuǐ) lái.*
May I have another (blanket)?	*Néng zài gěi wǒ (yì tiáo tǎnzi) ma?*
The room needs to be cleaned.	*Zhège fángjiān gāi dǎsǎo le.*
Could you vacuum the (rug)?	*Qǐng bǎ (dìtǎn) xī gānjìng.*
Please take this away.	*Qǐng bǎ zhèige ná zǒu.*
This plug doesn't fit.	*Zhèige chātóu chā bú shàng.*
What shall I do?	*Zěnme bàn?*

请在明天早晨六点叫醒我。

厕所坏了。

龙头漏水。

请帮我打开窗户。

这个门锁不上。

怎么开暖气？

这个电子表怎么调？

我的房间太吵了。

我想换一个房间。

我想要几条毛巾。

我想借一个熨斗。

请拿一瓶开水来。

能再给我一条毯子吗？

这个房间该打扫了。

请把地毯吸干净。

请把这个拿走。

这个插头插不上。

怎么办。

Post Office Tips

Here are some helpful hints for mailing letters in China:

● Envelopes are not pre-glued on the back flap, so be sure to seal your letters by using the glue provided at the post office or in your room. Licking the back of the envelope will not work.

● The smaller denominations of postage stamps, used on domestic mail, do not have glue on the back. Again, use the glue pot.

● When you mail a letter overseas, make sure the country of destination is clearly written; if possible, include the Chinese characters for that country.

English-language Publications

Several English-language magazines and one newspaper are published in China to inform foreign friends about China's viewpoints on national and international issues, its progress in the socialist construction, and general topics from sports to culture. Many hotels offer a selection of these publications free of charge. The well-known ones are:

China Daily

Founded in 1981, this is the only English-language newspaper published in China.

continued

Laundry

This is my laundry.	*Zhè shì wǒ yào xǐ de yīfu.*
When will I get my laundry back?	*Yīfu shénme shíhou néng xǐhǎo?*
Can it be done sooner?	*Néng kuài yìdiǎn ma?*
I need it (tonight).	*Wǒ (jīntiān wǎnshang) yào.*
This is to be (dry cleaned).	*Zhèi jiàn yào (gānxǐ).*
This should be (hand washed).	*Zhèi jiàn yào (yòng shǒu xǐ).*

Making a Phone Call

Where is the phone booth?	*Diànhuàtíng zài shénme dì fāng.*
I'd like to make a long-distance call to (the United States).	*Wǒ xiǎng gěi (Měiguó) dǎ yí gè chángtú diànhuà.*
Is there a public telephone near here?	*Fùjìn yǒu gōng yòng diànhuà ma?*
The number is: (123 456 7788).	*Hàomǎ shì (yī èr sān, sì wǔ liù, qī qī bā bā).*
How much does a call to (London) cost per minute?	*Gěi (Lúndūn) dǎ chángtú yì fēnzhōng duōshao qián?*
It's a collect call.	*Duìfāng fùkuǎn.*
I'll pay for the call.	*Wǒ fùkuǎn.*
I'll be using my credit card.	*Wǒ yòng xìnyòngkǎ fùkuǎn.*
I'd like to call (person to person).	*Wǒ yào dǎ gè (jiàorén) diànhuà.*
I placed my call (one hour) ago.	*Wǒ (yí gè xiǎoshí) yǐqián jiù yào guò diànhuà le.*
Could you see if I can get a line soon?	*Néng bāng wǒ kuài yìdiǎn jiētōng ma?*

这是我要洗的衣服。

衣服什么时候能洗好?

能快一点吗?

我今天晚上要。

这件要干洗。

这件要用手洗。

电话亭在什么地方?

我想给美国打一个长途电话。

附近有公用电话吗?

号码是:123 456 7788。

给伦敦打长途一分钟多少钱?

对方付款。

我付款。

我用信用卡付款。

我要打个叫人电话

我一个小时以前就要过电话了。

能帮我快一点接通吗?

Beijing Review

Established in 1958, this is China's only foreign-languange weekly devoted to news and politics.

China Pictorial

Founded in 1950, this highly illustrated magazine reports on China's socialist construction and the life of its many nationalities.

China Reconstructs

Founded by Soong Ching Ling (Mrs. Sun Yat-sen) to promote understanding and friendship between the Chinese people and the rest of the world, this comprehensive monthly was first published in 1952.

China Sports

Established in 1957, this monthly is devoted to the sports history and achievements of Chinese athletes.

Chinese Literature

First issued in 1951, this quarterly presents the translated works of modern Chinese writers as well as art and book reviews.

Women of China

First published in 1956, this monthly reports on achievements and issues concerning women.

Chinese-language Newspapers

What do the Chinese read very day? There are over 800 registered newspapers in China, published by various organizations at the national, provincial, municipal,

HOTEL

How much longer will I have to wait?	*Hái yào děng duōjiǔ?*
Your call didn't go through.	*Nǐ de diànhuà méiyǒu jiētōng.*
Please cancel the call I booked.	*Qǐng qǔxiāo gāngcái wǒ yào de diànhuà.*
Please give me extension (800).	*Qǐng jiē (bā líng líng) fēnjī.*
Please connect me with (the main desk).	*Qǐng jiē (zǒng fúwùtái).*
The line is not clear.	*Xiànlù bù qīngchǔ.*
It was a wrong number.	*Hàomǎ cuò le.*
My phone is out of order.	*Wǒde diànhuà chū gùzhàng le.*
Could you help me make a call?	*Nǐ néng bāng wǒ dǎ yí gè diànhuà ma?*
Do I need to dial "0" first?	*Yào xiān bō líng ma?*
Please connect me with the room of Mr. John.	*Qǐng bǎ diànhuà zhuǎn dào John xiānshēng de fángjiān*

The Foreign Exchange Desk

I'd like to convert (US dollars).	*Wǒ yào duìhuàn (Měiyuán).*
I have (traveler's checks).	*Wǒ yǒu (lǚxíng zhīpiào).*
Do you accept (credit cards)?	*Néng yòng (xìnyòngkǎ) ma?*
Please give me (large) bills.	*Qǐng gěi wǒ (dà) piàozi.*
Please give me (20 yuan) in small bills and change.	*Qǐng gěi wǒ (èrshí yuán) líng qián.*
May I have (a receipt)?	*Néng gěi wǒ (yì zhāng fāpiào) ma?*
Where can I get a cash advance on my credit card?	*Nǎr néng yòng xìnyòngkǎ duìhuàn xiànjīn?*

38

还要等多久？

你的电话没有接通。

请取消刚才我要的电话。

请接 800 分机。

请接总服务台。

线路不清楚。

号码错了。

我的电话出故障了。

你能帮我打一个电话吗？

要先拨"0"吗？

请把电话转到 John 先生的房间。

我要兑换美元。

我有旅行支票。

能用信用卡吗？

请给我大票子。

请给我二十元零钱。

能给我一张发票吗？

哪儿能用信用卡兑换现金？

and autonomous regional levels. The leading national newspapers are:

人民日报

Rénmín Rìbào (People's Daily)
This is the official newspaper of the CPC Central Committee. It began publication in 1947 in the North China Liberated Area.

光明日报

Guāngmíng Rìbào (Enlightenment Daily)
A newspaper mainly read by intellectuals, it began publication in 1949 as the organ of the All-China Democratic League and in 1952 became the combined organ of all the democratic parties.

经济日报

Jīngjì Rìbào (Economic Daily)
Founded in 1983, this newspaper reports on China's economic developments, reforms, products, and markets.

参考消息

Cānkǎo Xiāoxi (News Reference)
Widely read by people of all ages, this bulletin reports new developments in international politics and economy, with translations of articles from foreign presses. It originated as a pamphlet published in Yan'an in the 1930s.

体育报

Tǐyù Bào (Sports)
This is China's only nationwide sports newspaper. It is published twice a week by the State Physical Culture and Sports Commission. It began as a trial publication in 1956.

HOTEL

Where can I cash a (personal check)?

Zài nǎr néng duìhuàn (zhīpiào)?

Is this a (service fee)?

Zhè shì (fúwù fèi) ma?

What is the exchange rate?

Duìhuàn lǜ shì duōshao?

The Post Office

I'd like to mail (a letter).

Wǒ yào jì (xìn).

I'd like to buy (five) [80 fen] stamps.

Wǒ yào mǎi (wǔ) zhāng[bā máo] de yóupiào.

Please give me (three)[1.60 yuan] stamps.

Qǐng mài gěi wǒ (sān) zhāng [yí kuài liù] de yóupiào.

How much does it cost to mail a (postcard)?

Jì (míngxìnpiàn) yào duōshao qián?

Please send it (air mail).

Wǒ jì (hángkōng) xìn.

I want this letter sent by express.

Zhè fēng xìn wǒ yào jì tèkuàizhuāndì.

How long will it take this (package) to arrive?

Zhè (bāoguǒ) duōjiǔ néng dào?

Can you write the (name of the country) in Chinese for me?

Qǐng bāng wǒ bǎ (guó míng) xiě chéng Zhōngwén.

Can you help me wrap this?

Nǐ néng bāng wǒ bāo yíxià ma?

Do you have some (string)?

Yǒu (shéngzi) ma?

I would like to buy some (commemorative stamps).

Wǒ xiǎng mǎi yìxiē (jìniàn yóupiào).

Do you have (the whole set)?

Yǒu (quán tào de) ma?

When is the mail collected?

Yóudìyuán shénme shíjiān lái qǔ xìn?

Please send this parcel registered.

Qǐng yòng guàhào jì zhèige bāoguǒ

在哪儿能兑换支票?

这是服务费吗?

兑换率是多少?

我要寄信。

我要买五张八毛的邮票。

请卖给我三张一块六的邮票。

寄明信片要多少钱。

我寄航空信。

这封信我要寄特快专递。

这包裹多久能到?

请帮我把国名写成中文。

你能帮我包一下吗?

有绳子吗?

我想买一些纪念邮票。

有全套的吗?

邮递员什么时间来取信?

请用挂号寄这个包裹。

Tea

The most popular beverage in China is tea. Tea is said to have many curative effects, from improving eyesight and preventing tooth decay to helping reduce weight. Below are the names of the basic teas in China.

lùchá 绿茶
Green Tea: an unfermented tea with a clear taste and dark green color. The most famous green tea is West Lake Dragon Well Tea (*xīhú lóngjǐngchá*) produced in Hangzhou. It is known for its delicate taste.

hóngchá 红茶
Black Tea: a fermented tea with a fruit fragrance and mellow taste. A famous black tea is Keemun Tea (*qíhóng*) produced in Qimen, Anhui province. It has a sweet aftertaste.

wūlóngchá 乌龙茶
Oolong Tea: a semi-fermented tea produced in Fujian and Taiwan. A famous oolong tea is Iron Goddess of Mercy Tea (*tiěguān yīn chá*) which has a sweet aroma and concentrated taste.

huāchá 花茶
Scented Tea: a tea produced by smoke-processing tea leaves with flower petals. Jasmine Tea (*mòlìhuāchá*) is popular for its clear taste and jasmine fragrance.

zhuānchá 砖茶
Brick Tea: tea that is pressed into the shape of a brick, or other shape, after the tea leaves have been steamed. Easy to carry and store, this tea has a strong

Telegrams and Telexes

I'd like to send a (telegram) to [Guang zhou].
Wǒ xiǎng fā gè (diànbào) dào [Guǎngzhōu].

This is (the recipient's) name and address.
Zhè shì (duìfāng) de míngzi hé dìzhǐ.

This is the (cable address).
Zhè shì (diànbào guàhào).

Shall I write the (message) here?
(Nèiróng) shì xiě zài zhèr ma?

Please give me a copy of the (telex).
Qǐng gěi wǒ yí gè (diànchuán) fùběn.

Do you have a (fax machine)?
Yǒu (chuánzhēnjī) ma?

May I send it myself?
Wǒ kěyǐ zìjǐ fā ma?

I don't know how to use a (fax machine).
Wǒ bù zhīdao zěnme yòng (chuánzhēnjī).

The Barbershop

I need a (haircut).
Wǒ yào (lǐfà).

Please give me a (trim).
Qǐ bāng wǒ (xiūjiǎn) yíxià.

I'd like it rather (short).
Wǒ yào (duǎn) diǎn.

Please cut more (here).
(Zhè biān) duō jiǎn diǎn.

Please leave it long (here).
(Zhè biān) yào cháng diǎn.

Please do not use (conditioner).
Qǐng bú yào yòng (hùfàsù).

Please (blow dry) my hair.
Qǐng bǎ tóufà (chuīgān).

I'd like to have a (New Wave) look.
Wǒ xiǎng yào (xīncháo) fà shì.

我想发个电报到广州。

这是对方的名字和地址。

这是电报挂号。

内容是写在这儿吗?

请给我一个电传副本。

有传真机吗?

我可以自己发吗?

我不知道怎么用传真机。

我要理发。

请帮我修剪一下。

我要短点。

这边多剪点。

这边要长点。

请不要用护发素。

请把头发吹干。

我想要新潮发式。

taste and can dissolve fat. It is an indispensable beverage for nationalities that eat a lot of meat.

Batteries

Ran out of batteries? Don't worry, the common sizes of batteries are available in most local department stores. However, in China they are named not by alphabet but by number. Here's how to repuest the battery you want:

D battery (# 1)	*yī hào diànchí*
C battery (# 2)	*èr hào diànchí*
AA battery (# 5)	*wǔ hào diànchí*
AAA battery (# 7)	*qī hào diànchí*

What You'll hear

diànhuà fèi	telephone bill
diànhuà lái le	the call has come through
fúwùtái	service desk
fúwùyuán	service attendant
jǐ lóu	Which floor?
lóushàng	upstairs
lóuxià	downstairs
Méi rén jiē	No answer(phone)
Xiān bō líng	Dial "0" first.
zhàn xiàn	busy line (phone)

Signs

fàndiàn
Hotel

kāi mén
Open Door

guān mén
Close Door

lā
Pull

tuī
Push

Friends 5 五 wǔ

Chī le ma?
How's it going? (Eaten yet?)

In most places, you will get a warm and friendly response to your enthusiasm in speaking Chinese. A conversation can be struck and new acquaintances made with just a few simple words.

The most often used greeting, appropriate for all occasions, is *nǐhǎo* (hello). Around mealtimes, Chinese often greet each other with *Chī le* ma? (Have you eaten yet?) which is a general expression of concern for the other person. The proper reply, even if you haven't eaten for days, is *Chī le, xièxie* (I've eaten, thanks).

FRIENDS

Opening Lines

Hello.	*Nǐhǎo!*
How are you?	*Nǐ hǎo ma?*
(Fine), and you?	*(Hěn hǎo), nǐ ne?*
So-so.	*Hái kěyǐ.*
Not too bad.	*Bú cuò.*
Good morning.	*Zǎochén hǎo.*
Good evening.	*Wǎnshang hǎo.*
Good night.	*Wǎn'ān.*
How old are you? (to a child)	*Nǐ jǐ suì?*
How old are you? (adult)	*Nǐ jīnnián duōdà?*
I'm (twenty-five) years old.	*Wǒ (èrshí wǔ) suì.*
Where are you from?	*Nǐ shì nǎli rén?*
I'm from (England).	*Wǒ shì (Yīngguó) rén.*
What do you think of (Australia)?	*Nǐ duì (Àodàlìyà) de yìnxiàng rúhé?*
This is my first trip to (China).	*Wǒ shì dìyī cì lái (Zhōngguó).*
I would like to learn some (Chinese).	*Wǒ xiǎng xué yìxiē (Zhōngwén).*

Talk About the Weather

It's a (fine) day today.	*Jīntiān tiānqì (tǐng hǎo).*
God, It's really pouring!	*Āiyā, yǔ xià de zhēn dà!*
Do you know what the forecast for (tomorrow) is?	*Nǐ zhīdao (míngtiān) de tiānqì yùbào ma?*
The weather report says it will be (cold).	*Tiānqì yùbào shuō míngtiān huì (lěng).*
Tomorrow it might (rain).	*Míngtiān kěnéng (xià yǔ).*

你好!

你好吗?

很好,你呢?

还可以。

不错。

早晨好。

晚上好。

晚安。

你几岁?

你今年多大?

我二十五岁。

你是哪里人?

我是英国人。

你对澳大利亚的印象如何?

我是第一次来中国。

我想学一些中文。

今天天气挺好。

哎呀,雨下得真大!

你知道明天的天气预报吗?

天气预报说明天会冷。

明天可能下雨。

Chinese Names

Most Chinese names consist of two or three characters, or words, with the first being the surname. If a person is called Wang Zhonghua, for example, "Wang" is his family name and "Zhonghua" his given name. In Chinese culture, to call someone by his given name is a privilege reserved for family members and close friends. Therefore, to address someone politely, you should use either the full name, such as Wang Zhonghua. or the last name plus a title, such as *Wang lǎoshī* (Teacher Wang).

In informal situations, Chinese call each other by their last names preceded by *xiǎo* (young) or *lǎo* (old). For example, if Wang Zhonghua was a young man, he would be called Xiao Wang.

If the other person is not very familiar, Chinese often use the address *tóngzhì* (comrade) or, more respectfully, *shīfu* (master worker). In crowed stores, you will even hear the salesclerk being called *shīfu*, in hopes of faster service.

In China, the titles *xiānsheng* (Mr.), *tàitai* (Mrs.), and *xiǎojiě* (Miss) are often used.

(Psst... What'll I Call Him?)

If your friend's last name is Wang, how should you address him or her? Here are some suggestions for you to choose from, depending on Wang's age and status.

continued

FRIENDS

Talk About Family

Are you married?	*Nǐ jiéhūn le ma?*
Yes (I'm married).	*Jié le.*
No, not yet.	*Méi yǒu.*
I have (one) child.	*Wǒ yǒu (yí) gè háizi.*
Boy or girl?	*Shì nánháir háishì nǚháir?*
How old?	*Jǐ suì le?*
Do you have (brothers and sisters)?	*Nǐ yǒu (xiōngdì jiěmèi) ma?*
I have one (older sister).	*Wǒ yǒu yí gè (jiějie).*
Who are the members of your family?	*Nǐ jiā dōu yǒu shénme rén?*

Talk About Work

What do you do?	*Nǐ zuò shénme gōngzuò?*
I'm a (teacher).	*Wǒ shì (jiàoshī).*
Where do you (teach)?	*Nǐ zài nǎr (jiāoshū)?*
Are you satisfied with you (work)?	*Xǐhuan nǐde (gōngzuò) ma?*
It's not bad.	*Hái kěyǐ.*
I like (my work) very much.	*Wǒ fēicháng xǐhuan (wǒde gōngzuò).*
I'm considering (changing jobs).	*Wǒ zhèngzài kǎolǜ (diào gōngzuò) ne.*
I'm not very (satisfied).	*Bú tài (mǎnyì).*

Talk About Hobbies

What do you usually do in (your spare time)?	*Nǐ (yèyú shíjiān) gàn shénme?*

你结婚了吗?

结了。

没有。

我有一个孩子。

是男孩还是女孩?

几岁了?

你有兄弟姐妹吗?

我有一个姐姐。

你家都有什么人?

你做什么工作?

我是教师。

你在哪儿教书?

喜欢你的工作吗?

还可以。

我非常喜欢我的工作。

我正在考虑调工作呢。

不太满意。

你业余时间干什么?

elderly man	*Wang yéye*
elderly woman	*Wang nǎinai*
older person	*Lǎo Wang*

business or professional...

man	*Wang xiānsheng*
woman	*Wang nǚshì*
(Mrs.)	*Wang fūrén*
(Miss)	*Wang xiǎojiě*
young person	*Xiǎo Wang*
Driver	*Wang shīfu*
Bureau Director	*Wang júzhǎng*
School Principal	*Wang xiàozhǎng*
Manager	*Wang jīnglǐ*

Chinese Idioms

There are many four-word idioms in Chinese known as *chéngyǔ* (set phrase), which are sayings originated from folk stories. Because each *chéngyǔ* is a concise way of conveying a poignant meaning, Chinese use them often in everyday conversation. When the situation is ripe, delight your friends with these favorites.

老马识途 *Lǎo mǎ shí tú*
(old horse knows road)
Let experience take over.

熟能生巧 *Shú néng shēng qiǎo*
(mature ability brings skill)
Practice makes perfect.

亡羊补牢 *Wáng yáng bǔ láo*
(lost sheep mend fold)
Making repairs after the damage: better late than never.

掩耳盗铃 *Yǎn ěr dào líng*
(cover ears steal bell)
You're only fooling yourself.

continued

49

FRIENDS

I usually (read books).	*Wǒ jīngcháng (kàn shū).*
I like to (play soccer).	*Wǒ xǐhuan (tī zúqiú).*
What are you most (interested in)?	*Nǐ zuì (gǎnxìngqù) de shì shénme?*
I'm especially interested in (music).	*Wǒ duì (yīnyuè) tèbié gǎnxìngqù.*

Talk About Politics

Are you satisfied with China's present (economic) policy?	*Nǐ duì zhōngguó mùqián de (jīngjì) zhèngcè mǎnyì ma?*
What areas are currently undergoing reform?	*Mùqián yǒu nǎ xiē lǐngyù zài shíxíng gǎigé?*
Do you think China's present (urban) reform is making progress?	*Nǐ rènwéi Zhōngguó mùqián de (chéngshì) gǎigé qǔdé jìnzhǎn le ma?*
Do most Chinese join the (Communist Party of China)?	*Shìfǒu dàduōshù Zhōngguó rén dōu jiārù (Zhōngguó Gòngchǎndǎng)?*
Out of every ten (young people) how many are [Party members]?	*Měi shí gè (niánqīng rén) zhōng, yǒu jǐ gè shì [Dǎng yuán]?*
Does (everyone) take part in elections?	*(Měigè rén) dōu cānjiā xuǎnjǔ ma?*
What do you think of (American) foreign policy?	*Nǐ duì (Měiguó) de wàijiāo zhèngcè zěnme kàn?*

Saying Good-bye

I'm very pleased to have met you.	*Rènshi nǐ hěn gāoxìng.*
It's been nice talking with you.	*Hěn gāoxìng néng hé nǐ jiāotán.*
Good-bye. (See you again.)	*Zàijiàn.*

我经常看书。

我喜欢踢足球。

你最感兴趣的是什么？

我对音乐特别感兴趣。

你对中国目前的经济政策满意吗？

目前有哪些领域在实行改革？

你认为中国目前的城市改革取得进展了吗？

是否大多数中国人都加入中国共产党？

每十个年轻人中有几个是党员？

每个人都参加选举吗？

你对美国的外交政策怎么看？

认识你很高兴。

很高兴能和你交谈。

再见。

一箭双雕 *Yí jiàn shuāng diāo*
(one arrow two hawks)
Killing two birds with one stone.

Seeing off a Friend

It is an age-old custom in China to see friends to the gate when they leave one's home. Many classic poems, in fact, describe the sadness of that moment of final parting. Here are some phrases that are still used every time a guest leaves.

Wǒ sòng sòng nǐ.	Let me see you off.
Bú sòng, bú sòng.	No, no, it's not necessary.
Méi guānxi, méi guānxi.	It's nothing, don't worry.
Qǐng liúbù.	Please don't trouble —this is far enough.
Shù bù yuǎn sòng.	All right, pardon my not seeing you out farther.

What You'll Hear

bù hǎoyìsi	feel embarrassed
Bú jiàn bú sàn.	I'll be there. Don't leave without me.
Chōuyān ma?	Do you smoke?
gòuqiàng	not likely
Hǎo jiǔ bú jiàn.	Long time no see.
huānyíng	welcome
Jiùshì!	Precisely!
Jiù zhèyàng ba.	That's settled, then.
Zāo gāo le.	It's a disaster.
Zěnme huí shì(r)?	What happened here?

Signs

讲文明 讲礼貌 讲卫生 讲纪律 讲道德

讲文明

jiǎng wénmíng
Be Civilized

讲礼貌

jiǎng lǐmào
Be Polite

讲卫生

jiǎng wèishēng
Be Cleanly

讲纪律

jiǎng jìlǜ
Be Orderly

讲道德

jiǎng dàodé
Be Moral

Food **6** 六
liù

Wèidao hǎo jí le!
Delicious!

Hungry? Need a quick pickup? Dying for a hamburger? Not to worry – China offers some of the best food in the world, if only you know where to find it and how to ask for it. You can find food on the train, in the hotel, at a snack stall, and, of course, in a restaurant. Whether you're buying a bowl of noodles or ordering a twenty-course banquet, the phrases in this chapter will help you make clear what you want.

FOOD

Eating on the Run

I'm thirsty.	*Wǒ kě le.*
I'm hungry.	*Wǒ è le.*
I'm starving.	*Wǒ è sǐ le.*
Where can I get something to eat?	*Nǎr yǒu mài chī de?*
Where can I buy a (cold drink)?	*Nǎr mài (lěngyǐn)?*
(Two) bottles of [beer], please.	*Qǐng lái (liǎng) píng [píjiǔ].*
I'd like a cup of (coffee).	*Wǒ yào yì bēi (kāfēi).*
Please give me a bowl of (noodles).	*Qǐng lái yì wǎn (miàntiáo).*
How much is this?	*Zhège duōshao qián?*
Give me (one), please.	*Qǐng gěi wǒ (yí) gè.*
Can I have a doggy bag, please.	*Wǒ kěyǐ dǎ bāo ma?*
Do I need to return the (bottle)?	*Yào tuì (píng) ma?*
I'm leaving the (bowl) here.	*Wǒ bǎ (wǎn) fàng zài zhèr.*
Do I get back a (deposit)?	*Yǒu (yājīn) ma?*

Finding a Place to Eat

where is there a good (restaurant)?	*Nǎr yǒu hǎo yìdiǎn de (fànguǎn)?*
Is it (expensive)?	*(Guì) bú (guì)?*
I would like to go to a (Sichuan) restaurant.	*Wǒ xiǎng qù yì jiā (Sìchuān) cāntīng.*
We would like a simple meal.	*Wǒmen xiǎng chī jiǎndān yìdiǎn.*

What's for Breakfast?

我渴了。

我饿了。

我饿死了。

哪儿有卖吃的?

哪儿卖冷饮?

请来两瓶啤酒。

我要一杯咖啡。

请来一碗面条。

这个多少钱?

请给我一个。

我可以打包吗?

要退瓶吗?

我把碗放在这儿。

有押金吗?

哪儿有好一点的饭馆?

贵不贵?

我想去一家四川餐厅。

我们想吃简单一点。

Chinese rarely have bacon and eggs for breakfast. Instead, they have a bowl of hot rice congee with a few pickled vegetables or other side dishes. On the run, instead of a doughnut and coffee, Chinese have **yóutiáo** (fried cruller) and **dòujiāng** (soybean milk). If you'd like to try breakfast Chinese-style, ask a local friend where to find these favorite items:

包子	**bāozi**
	steamed dumpling
大米粥	**dàmǐzhōu**
	rice congee
豆浆	**dòujiāng**
	soybean milk
豆沙包	**dòushābāo**
	steamed bean-paste dumpling
煎饼	**jiānbǐng**
	crepe (with cruller)
泡菜	**pàocài**
	pickled vegetables
肉松	**ròusōng**
	shredded dried meat
烧饼	**shāobǐng**
	sesame seed biscuit
汤面	**tāng miàn**
	soup noodles
咸鸭蛋	**xián yādàn**
	salted duck egg
油条	**yóutiáo**
	fried cruller
榨菜	**zhàcài**
	hot pickled mustard
炸糕	**zhágāo**
	fried sticky-rice cake

FOOD

I'm dying for a (Western meal).	*Wǒ fēicháng xiǎng chī (Xīcān).*
There's a (fast-food place) nearby.	*Fùjìn yǒu yì jiā (kuàicān diàn).*
Let's go.	*Zǒu ba.*

Making Reservations

I'd like to make a reservation for (Tuesday) night.	*Wǒ xiǎng yùdìng (xīngqī èr) wǎnshang de fàn.*
We'll arrive at (7:30).	*Wǒmen (qī diǎn bàn) lái.*
There will be (four) people.	*(Sì) gè rén.*
I'd like to pay (forty) yuan per person.	*Měi rén (sì shí) yuán.*
Will you be able to accommodate us?	*Nǐmen néng jiēdài ma?*
What time would be better?	*Shénme shíjiān jiào hǎo?*
How much is it per person?	*Měi rén duōshao qián?*
Are beverages included?	*Bāokuò yǐnliào ma?*
Is there anything (cheaper)?	*Yǒu (piányi yìdiǎn) de ma?*
Okay, that'll do.	*Hǎo, jiù zhèyàng.*
See you (Tuesday).	*(Xīngqī èr) jiàn.*

Getting a Table

A party of (three).	*Wǒmen (sān) gè rén.*
A table for (two), please.	*(Liǎng) gè rén zuò nǎr?*
There's a draft here.	*Zhèr yǒu fēng.*
Could we switch to another table?	*Néng huàn gè zhuōzi ma?*
May we sit over there?	*Néng zuò zài nàr ma?*

我非常想吃西餐。

附近有一家快餐店。

走吧!

我想预定星期二晚上的饭。

我们七点半来。

四个人。

每人四十元。

你们能接待吗?

什么时间较好?

每人多少钱?

包括饮料吗?

有便宜一点的吗?

好,就这样。

星期二见。

我们三个人。

两个人坐哪儿?

这儿有风。

能换个桌子吗?

能坐在那儿吗?

What's for Dinner?

You've finally found a place to eat. You're seated at the table, and the waiter has handed you the menu. Now what? If you are puzzled by the menu at hand, try pointing to some of the choices below and asking *Yǒu méi yǒu zhèige*? (Do you have this?) The items here are standard dishes available at most restaurants.

香酥鸡	*xiāngsūjī*	crispy fried chicken
宫保鸡丁	*gōngbǎo jīdīng*	hot spicy chicken with peanuts
糖醋鱼	*tángcù yú*	sweet-and-sour fish
红烧鱼	*hóngshāo yú*	braised fish in brown sauce
木须肉	*mùxu ròu*	mushu pork
鱼香肉丝	*yúxiāng ròusī*	pork in hot garlic sauce
葱头炒牛肉	*cōngtóu chǎo niúròu*	beef with onions
麻婆豆腐	*mápó dòufu*	hot spicy beancurd
砂锅豆腐	*shāguō dòufu*	beancurd casserole
香菇冬笋	*xiānggū dōngsǔn*	black mushrooms and bamboo
蘑菇菜心	*mógu càixīn*	Chinese cabbage with mushrooms
炒豆芽	*chǎo dòuyá*	sauteed bean sprouts
酸辣汤	*suānlà tāng*	hot-and-sour soup

continued

FOOD

Ordering

Waiter!	*Fúwùyuán!*
Miss!	*Xiǎojiě!*
The menu, please.	*Qǐng gěi wǒmen càidān.*
What is the house specialty?	*Zhèr yǒu shénme míng cài?*
What regional cuisine do your serve here?	*Zhèr yǒu shénme fēngwèi cài?*
Do you have (Peking Duck)?	*Yǒu (kǎoyā) ma?*
Can you recommend some dishes?	*Nǐ néng tuījiàn yìxiē cài ma?*
I like (chicken).	*Wǒ xǐhuan chī (jī).*
My favorite food is (shrimp).	*Wǒ zuì ài chī (xiā).*
I don't like (mushrooms).	*Wǒ bù xǐhuan (mógu).*
I don't eat (pork).	*Wǒ bù chī (zhūròu).*
I'm vegetarian.	*Wǒ zhǐ chī sùcài.*
I'm allergic to (seafood).	*Wǒ chī (hǎixiān) huì guòmǐn.*
Please order more (vegetables).	*Qǐng duō lái jǐ pán (shūcài).*
What (soups) do you have?	*Yǒu shénme (tāng)?*
Is the (fish) fresh?	*(Yú) xīnxiān ma?*
Please leave out the (MSG).	*Qǐng bú yào fàng (wèijīng).*
Please don't make it too (spicy).	*Bú yào tài (là).*
May I order now?	*Kěyǐ diǎncài le ma?*
I'll have...	*Wǒ yào...*
one (homestyle beancurd)	*yí gè (jiācháng dòufu)*
(two) bowls of rice	*(liǎng) wǎn mǐfàn*
a pot of (jasmine) tea	*yì hú (mòlìhuā) chá*

58

服务员！

小姐！

请给我们菜单。

这儿有什么名菜？

这儿有什么风味
菜？

有北京烤鸭吗？

你能推荐一些菜
吗？

我喜欢吃鸡。

我最爱吃虾。

我不喜欢蘑菇。

我不吃猪肉。

我只吃素菜。

我吃海鲜会过敏。

请多来几盘蔬菜。

有什么汤？

鱼新鲜吗？

请不要放味精。

不要太辣。

可以点菜了吗？

我要……

一个家常豆腐

两碗米饭

一壶茉莉花茶。

米饭	*mǐfàn*	rice
馒头	*mántou*	steamed roll

Local Snacks

As you travel throughout China, you will have the chance to sample many local snacks. Below are some of the most popular snacks in four major cities.

Beijing

冰糖葫芦	*bīngtáng húlu*	candied haws on a stick
涮羊肉	*shuànyángròu*	Mongolian hot pot
豌豆黄	*wāndòuhuáng*	pea-flour cake
杏仁茶	*xìngrénchá*	almond-flour tea
羊肉串	*yángròuchuàn*	mutton shish kebab

Shanghai

豆沙包	*dòushābāo*	sweet bean-paste dumplings
馄饨	*húndùn*	wontons
小笼包	*xiǎolóngbāo*	small steamed dumplings
芝麻汤团	*zhīma tāngtuán*	sesame sweet-rice dumplings in soup

Xi'an

饸饹	*héle*	buckwheat spaghetti
面皮	*miànpí*	flat noodles made of

continued

59

FOOD

During the meal.

That's not what I ordered.	*Zhè bú shì wǒ diǎn de cài.*
I asked for (curried chicken).	*Wǒ yào de shì (gālí Jī).*
This is too (salty).	*Zhèige tài (xián) le.*
This is not (fresh).	*Zhèige bù (xīnxiān).*
The food is (cold).	*Cài (liáng) le.*
What (meat) is this?	*Zhè shì shénme (ròu)?*
May we have some (forks)?	*Néng gěi wǒmen jǐgè (chāzi) ma?*
Do you have any (hot sauce)?	*Yǒu (làjiàng) ma?*
We need some (napkins).	*Wǒmen yào (cānjīnzhǐ).*
This dish is (excellent).	*Zhège cài (hǎo chī jí le).*
Can you write down the (name of the dish) for me?	*Nǐ néng bāng wǒ xiě xià (cài míng) ma?*

Ending the Meal

We have finished.	*Chī wán le.*
Check, please.	*Jiézhàng ba.*
That was a (very good) meal	*Zhè dùn fàn chī de (hěn hǎo).*
We enjoyed it.	*Wǒmen hěn mǎnyì.*

这不是我点的菜。

我要的是咖喱鸡。

这个太咸了。

这个不新鲜。

菜凉了。

这是什么肉?

能给我们几个叉子吗?

有辣酱吗?

我们要餐巾纸。

这个菜好吃极了。

你能帮我写下菜名吗?

吃完了。

结帐吧。

这顿饭吃得很好。

我们很满意。

		steamed refined wheat dough, served with sauces and seasonings
柿子饼	*shìzibǐng*	fried persimmon cake
羊肉泡馍	*yángròu pàomó*	crumbled unleavened bread soaked in lamb stew

Guangzhou

春卷	*chūnjuǎn* (chun kuen)	spring roll
烧麦	*shāomai* (siu mai)	steamed pork dumpling
虾饺	*xiājiǎo* (ha kaau)	shrimp dumplings
鲜荷叶饭	*xiān héyè fàn* (sin haw mai faan)	rice wrapped in fresh lotus leaf
炸虾球	*zháxiāqiú* (cha ha k'ow)	fried shrimp balls

*Cantonese pronunciations are in parentheses.

What You'll Hear

Gānbēi!	Cheers! Bottoms up.
Hái yào shénme?	Would you like anything else?
Jǐ wèi?	How many people?
Nǐmen xiǎng hē shénme?	What would you like to drink?
Nǐmen yùdìng le ma?	Do you have a reservation?
Qǐng jiézhàng.	Please pay the bill.
Yào mǐfàn ma?	Do you want rice?
Zhù nǐ jiànkāng!	To your health!

FOOD

Signs

cāntīng
**Dining Hall,
Restaurant**

lěngyǐn rèyǐn
**Cold and Hot
Drinks**

yān jiǔ shípǐn
**Cigarettes,
Liquor,
Foodstuffs**

shuǐjiǎo
**Boiled
Dumplings**

miàntiáo
Noodles

62

Sightseeing 7 七 qī

Tài bàng le!
Wow! Too much!

China abounds with scenic, historic, and cultural attractions, as well as factories and schools to visit. You will have questions to ask and comments to make at each site. Whether seeking facts or simply asking someone to move aside for a photograph, it will be invaluable to know a few words of chinese.

SIGHTSEEING

Planning Your Excursion

Can you tell me where the (China International Travel Service) is?

Nǐ néng gàosù wǒ (Zhōngguó Guójì Lǚxíng Shè) zài nǎr ma?

I need an English-speaking (guide).

Wǒ xūyào yí gè Yīngyǔ (dǎoyóu).

What will be the fee per (hour)?

Měi (xiǎoshí) duōshao qián?

Can you arrange a trip to (Xi'an)?

Néng ānpái dào (Xī'ān) lǚxíng ma?

Can you recommend a (sightseeing tour)?

Néng tuījiàn yì tiáo (guānguāng lùxiàn) ma?

I want to see some (scenic spots).

Wǒ xiǎng kàn yìxiē (fēngjǐng diǎn).

I would like to visit a (factory).

Wǒ xiǎng cānguān yí gè (gōngchǎng).

Do you have a (local) map?

Yǒu (dāngdì) dìtú ma?

What are the (places of interest) in this city?

Zhèige chéngshì yǒu shénme (kě kàn de dìfang)?

What is the itinerary?

Lǚyóu rìchéng shì zěnme ānpái de?

Are we going by (bus)?

Shì zuò (qìchē) qù ma?

How long will the ride be?

Zuò chē yào duōjiǔ?

When do we set out?

Shénme shíhou chūfā?

At the Site

What (park) is this?

Zhè shì shénme (gōngyuán)?

When was this (palace) built?

Zhèige (gōngdiàn) shì shénme shíhou jiàn de?

Symbols

你能告诉我中国国际旅行社在哪儿吗？

我需要一个英语导游。

每小时多少钱？

能安排到西安旅行吗？

能推荐一条观光路线吗？

我想看一些风景点。

我想参观一个工厂。

有当地地图吗？

这个城市有什么可看的地方？

旅游日程是怎么安排的？

是坐汽车去吗？

坐车要多久？

什么时候出发？

这是什么公园？

这个宫殿是什么时候建的？

Chinese art is full of symbolic images – you will often see dragons, or peaches, or plum blossoms on paintings, architecture, textiles, and decorative objects. What do these motifs stand for? Below are some of the traditional symbols and their meanings.

bat: luck
chrysanthemum: nobility, purity
crane: longevity
dragon: the emperor: China
lion: power, dignity
lotus: purity, continuity
mandarin ducks: marital harmony
peach: long life, immortality
peony: wealth, honor
phoenix: the empress
pine tree: longevity
plum blossom: transience, delicacy
tiger: guardian against evil
tortoise: longevity

Flowers

China's vast territory extends across the frigid, temperate, and tropical zones, making it possible for a great variety of plant species. Below are the names of some common flowers in China. Use this list when asking a local friend *zhè shì shénme huā*? (What flower is this?)

茶花	*cháhuā*	camelia
杜鹃花	*dùjuānhuā*	azalea
凤仙花	*fèngxiānhuā*	touch-me-not
桂花	*guìhuā*	cassia

continued

SIGHTSEEING

How large is (Tian'anmen Square)?	(*Tiān'ānmén Guǎngchǎng*) *duōdà*?
How high is this (pagoda)?	*Zhèige* (*tǎ*) *duōgāo*?
What does this (lion) symbolize?	*Zhèige* (*shīzi*) *dàibiǎo shénme*?
Whom does this picture portray?	*Zhèi zhāng huà huà de shì shéi*?
What other (temples) can I visit?	*Hái yǒu shénme* (*sìmiào*) *kě kàn*?
How long will we stay here?	*Wǒmen yào zài zhèr dāi duōjiǔ*?
I want to buy some (souvenirs).	*Wǒ xiǎng mǎi yìxiē* (*jìniàn pǐn*).

At the Zoo

I would like to see the (giant pandas).	*Wǒ xiǎng kàn* (*dàxióngmāo*).
Where is its habitat?	*Tā zhù zài shénme dìfang*?
What does (it) eat?	(*Tā*) *chī shénme*?
How many cubs does the (panda) have in one brood?	(*Xióngmāo*) *yì tāi shēng jǐge*?
How old is this (panda)?	*Zhèige* (*xióngmāo*) *duōdà le*?

At the Factory

May I ask a few questions?	*Wǒ kěyǐ wèn jǐge wèntí ma*?
What are your products?	*Nǐmen yǒu shénme chǎnpǐn*?
How many (workers) do you have?	*Nǐmen yǒu duōshao* (*gōngrén*)?
How long does it take to complete (one carpet)?	*Zuò* (*yí kuài dìtǎn*) *yào duōcháng shíjiān*?

天安门广场多大?		
这个塔多高?		
这个狮子代表什么?		
这张画画的是谁?		
还有什么寺庙可看?		
我们要在这儿呆多久?		
我想买一些纪念品。		
我想看大熊猫。		
它住在什么地方?		
它吃什么?		
熊猫一胎生几个?		
这个熊猫多大了?		
我可以问几个问题吗?		
你们有什么产品?		
你们有多少工人?		
做一块地毯要多长时间?		

荷花	*héhuā*	lotus
鸡冠花	*jīguānhuā*	cock's comb
夹竹桃	*jiāzhútáo*	oleander
腊梅	*làméi*	allspice
兰花	*lánhuā*	orchid
茉莉	*mòli*	jasmine
牡丹	*mǔdan*	tree peony
蔷薇	*qiángwēi*	hedge rose
秋海棠	*qiūhǎitáng*	begonia
芍药	*sháoyao*	peony
水浮莲	*shuǐfúlián*	water lily
水仙	*shuǐxiān*	narcissus
绣球	*xiùqiú*	geranium
月季	*yuèjì*	Chinese rose

Trees

China observes arbor day on March 12, when young trees are planted all across the country. In southern towns, shade trees often line both sides of the streets, providing refuge from the summer heat. When identifying the trees you see, refer to the list below.

白果树	*báiguǒshù*	gingko
白杨树	*báiyángshù*	aspen
柏树	*bǎishù*	cypress
松树	*sōngshù*	pine
丁香树	*dīngxiāngshù*	lilac
核桃树	*hétaoshù*	walnut
槐树	*huáishù*	locust
柳树	*liǔshù*	willow
榕树	*róngshù*	banyan
桑树	*sāngshù*	mulberry
石榴树	*shíliushù*	pomegranate
柿子树	*shìzishù*	persimmon

continued

SIGHTSEEING

How long did you train for this job?	*Nǐ xué guò duōjiǔ?*
Do you have a (labor union)?	*Nǐmen yǒu (gōnghuì) ma?*
Do you use a (bonus system)?	*Nǐmen yǒu (jiǎngjīn zhìdù) ma?*
What is the monthly salary of a (worker)?	*(Gōngrén) měi yuè gōngzī duōshao?*
What are your working hours?	*Nǐmen měi tiān jǐdiǎn shàngxià bān?*
What is your work quota per (day)?	*Měi (tiān) de gōngzuò liàng shì duōshao?*

Taking a Photo

Can I take a picture here?	*Néng zài zhèr zhàoxiàng ma?*
Do you mind if I photograph you?	*Kěyǐ gěi nǐ zhào zhāng xiàng ma?*
Would you take a picture for me, please?	*Nǐ néng tì wǒ zhào zhāng xiàng ma?*
Everything is set.	*Dōu tiáo hǎo le.*
Just press the button.	*Zhǐ yào àn kuàimén jiù xíng le.*
Excuse me, please move aside.	*Duìbuqǐ, qǐng ràng yíxià.*
We want to take a picture here.	*Wǒmen xiǎng zài zhèr zhào zhāng xiàng.*
Please give me your address.	*Qǐng gěi wǒ nǐde dìzhǐ.*
I'll send you (the photos) later.	*Yǐhòu wǒ bǎ (zhàopiàn) gěi nǐ jì qù.*

你学过多久？

你们有工会吗？

你们有奖金制度吗？

工人每月工资多少？

你们每天几点上下班？

每天的工作量是多少？

能在这儿照相吗？

可以给你照张相吗？

你能替我照张相吗？

都调好了。

只要按快门就行了。

对不起，请让一下。

我们想在这儿照张相。

请给我你的地址。

以后我把照片给你寄去。

桃树	*táoshù*	peach
梧桐树	*wútóngshù*	Chinese parasol
柚子树	*yòuzishù*	pomelo
榆树	*yúshù*	elm
樟树	*zhāngshù*	camphor

Zoo Animals

When you visit zoos in China, you will see a few animals that are not often found in Western zoos. The all-time favorite, of course, is the giant panda. Here are the names of some animals particular to China.

大熊猫	*dàxióngmāo*	giant panda
丹顶鹤	*dāndǐnghè*	red-crowned crane
金丝猴	*jīnsīhóu*	golden-haired monkey
滩羊	*tānyáng*	argali sheep
小熊猫	*xiǎo-xióngmāo*	lesser panda

What You'll Hear

Dōu dào le.	We're all here.
Guānmén le.	It's closed.
Jīntiān xiūxi.	Today is the day off.
lǎowài	foreigner (slang)
ménpiào	admission ticket
míngxìnpiàn	postcard
wàibīn	foreign guest
wàiguórén	foreigner
Xiǎoxīn!	Careful!
Yánjìn pāizhào.	Photography prohibited.

Signs

huānyíng
Welcome

shòu piào chù
Ticket Office

ménpiào: 2 yuán
Admission: 2 *yuán*

bù zhǔn suídì tùtán
No Spitting

yóukè zhǐ bù
Visitors Keep Out

八 bā 8 Shopping

Duōshao qián?
How much?

Shopping in China outside the Friendship Stores and other shops catering to foreign tourists is like treasure-hunting in a jungle. The hunt will be much easier if you can describe what you want and, more importantly, get the attention of the salesclerk.

In the many free markets that have sprung up all over China, the key phrase after *Duōshao qián?* (How much?) is *Tài guì le* (too expensive). In nongovernment stores, especially high-priced souvenir shops, you can try *Néng piányi yìdiǎn ma?* (Can the price be lowered?) Then be prepared to bargain!

SHOPPING

Scouting the Market

Where can I buy some souvenirs?	*Nǎli kěyǐ mǎi dào jìniànpǐn ne?*
Where is the nearest (arts and crafts store)?	*Zuìjìn de (gōngyì měishù shāngdiàn) zài nǎr?*
Can you recommend a (department store)?	*Nǐ néng jièshào yí gè (bǎihuò shāngdiàn) ma?*
I would like to buy some (silk fabric).	*Wǒ xiǎng mǎi diǎn (sīchóu).*
Can you accompany me to the (free market)?	*Nǐ néng péi wǒ qù (zìyóu shìchǎng) ma?*
When does it open?	*Shénme shíhou kāimén?*

Making the Find

Comrade!	*Tóngzhì!*
Miss!	*Xiǎojiě!*
Can you help me?	*Qǐng bāng yíxià máng.*
I'd like to take a look at this (jacket).	*Wǒ xiǎng kàn yíxià zhèi jiàn (jiākè shān).*
Do you have any (others)?	*Yǒu (qítā) de ma?*
I'm looking for (cloisonne vases).	*Wǒ xiǎng mǎi (jǐngtàilán huāpíng).*
This has a (flaw).	*Zhèige yǒu (máobìng).*
Please show me (that one).	*Qǐng gěi wǒ (nèige) kànkan.*
Is this (handmade)?	*Zhè shì (shǒugōng zuò de) ma?*
What kind of fabric is this?	*Zhè shì shénme liàozi de?*
Where is it made?	*Nǎr chǎn de?*
How much is it?	*Duōshao qián?*
Can you bring the price down?	*Néng piányi diǎn ma?*

Cashier's Booth

Many local stores have a cashier's booth where you must pay for your purchase before picking it up at the sales counter. When you have decided what to buy, the salesclerk at the counter will write out a bill and give you two copies. Take those copies to the cashier's booth, pay the amount shown, and return with a stamped copy of the bill as your receipt. When you hand the receipt to the salesclerk, he or she will give you your goods.

Special Items

The true shopper cannot be deterred, language barrier or not. If you wish to buy a few special Chinese items but have difficulty telling the store clerk what you want, try pointing to the list below. (Refer to the dictionary section for pronunciations.)

哪里可以买到纪念品呢？

最近的工艺美术商店在哪儿？

你能介绍一个百货商店吗？

我想买点丝绸。

你能陪我去自由市场吗？

什么时候开门？

同志！

小姐！

请帮一下忙。

我想看一下这件夹克衫。

有其他的吗？

我想买景泰蓝花瓶。

这个有毛病。

请给我那个看看。

这是手工做的吗？

这是什么料子的？

哪儿产的？

多少钱？

能便宜点吗？

竹编	bambooware (woven)
蜡染	batik
织锦	brocade
中山装	cadre's jacket
毛笔	calligraphy brush
地毯	carpet
开士米毛衣	cashmere sweater
旗袍	cheongsam (gown)
图章	chop (seal)
泥人	clay figurine
景泰蓝	cloisonne
棉衣	cotton-padded jacket
棉鞋	cotton-padded shoes
双面绣	double-sided embroidery
折扇	folding fan

continued

SHOPPING

Closing the Deal

Okay, I'll take it.	*Hǎo, jiù yào tā.*
It's too expensive.	*Tài guì le.*
Can you give me a discount?	*Kěyǐ dǎ gè zhékòu ma?*
I don't want it.	*Wǒ bú yào.*
Could you wrap it for me, please?	*Qǐng bāo yíxià, hǎo ma?*
Please wrap each separately.	*Qǐng fēn kāi bāo.*
Do you have a (box) for it?	*Yǒu (hézi) ma?*
Please give me a (receipt).	*Qǐng gěi wǒ (fāpiào).*

Art and Antiques

Is this an (original)?	*Zhè shì (yuánzuò) ma?*
Is the (calligrapher) still living?	*Zhèige (shūfǎjiā) hái huózhe ma?*
Would you write down the artist's (brief background)?	*Néng bǎ zhèige yìshùjiā de (jiǎndān qíngkuàng) xiě gěi wǒ ma?*
Do you sell (reproductions)?	*Zhèr mài (fùzhìpǐn) ma?*
When was this made?	*Zhè shì shénme niándài de?*
What dynasty does it date from?	*Tā shì nǎge cháodài de?*
I must have one with a red wax seal on it.	*Wǒ yào yí gè dǎguò huǒqī yìn de.*
I won't be able to take this (out of the country).	*Zhèige wǒ bù néng dài (chū jìng).*

Books

I'm looking for a (good) English-Chinese dictionary.	*Wǒ xiǎng mǎi yì běn (hǎo) de Yīng-Hàn zìdiǎn.*

皮帽子	fur hat
砚台	ink slab
墨	ink stick
铁花	iron openwork
玉雕	jade carving
漆器	lacquerware
瓷器	porcelain
军帽	Mao cap
军便服	Mao jacket
鼻烟壶	miniature bottle painting
微雕	miniature carving
剪纸	papercut
珍珠霜	pearl cream
印泥	red paste for seals
宣纸	rice paper
檀香扇	sandalwood fan
皮影	shadow puppet
贝雕画	shell mosaic
丝绸	silk fabric
丝绸睡袍	silk robe
拓片	stone rubbings
壁毯	tapestry
清凉油	tiger balm
鸭舌帽	worker's cap

好，就要它。

太贵了。

可以打个折扣吗？

我不要。

请包一下好吗？

请分开包。

有盒子吗？

请给我发票。

这是原作吗？

这个书法家还活着吗？

能把这个艺术家的简单情况写给我吗？

这儿卖复制品吗？

这是什么年代的？

它是哪个朝代的？

我要一个打过火漆印的。

这个我不能带出境。

我想买一本好的英汉字典。

Buying Jade

The main factors that go into the price of a piece of jade are the material used, the carving skill, and the color. In the Chinese jade industry, the materials are grouped into three categories. They are:

féicuì 翡翠
Chrysolite. The most valuable jade, its color appears green but on close inspection can be seen to have both white and green elements.

continued

SHOPPING

Where are the (children's) books?	(Értóng) shū zài nǎr?
I'm looking for a book about Chinese (youth).	Wǒ xiǎng mǎi yì běn guānyú zhōngguó (qīngnián) de shū.
I'm looking for works by (Lu Xun).	Wǒ xiǎng mǎi (Lǔ Xùn) de zuòpǐn.
Do you have (this book)?	Yǒu (zhè běn shū) ma?

Clothing

Can I try it on?	Néng shì yíxià ma?
Do you have a (large)?	Yǒu (dà hào) de ma?
Is there a (mirror)?	Yǒu (jìngzi) ma?
Please show me a (smaller) one.	Yǒu (xiǎo yìdiǎn) de ma?
I'd like something (brighter).	Wǒ xǐhuan (yánsè xiānyàn yìdiǎn) de.
I wear size (42).	Wǒ chuān (sìshi èr) hào.
This pair of pants doesn't fit me.	Zhè tiáo chángkù bù hé wǒ shēn.
It is little (loose) around the waist.	Yāo bù sōng le yìxiē.
May I see some others in different colors?	Wǒ kěyǐ kàn qítā bùtóng yánsè de ma?
Will this sweater shrink any when washed?	zhè jiàn máoyī xǐ le huì bú huì suō shuǐ?

Film

I'd like to buy an automatic camera.	Wǒ xiǎng mǎi jià quán zìdòng zhàoxiàngjī.
I'd like (two) rolls of [color-print film].	Wǒ xiǎng mǎi (liǎng) gè [cǎijuǎn].
(36) exposures	(sānshí liù) zhāng de

儿童书在哪儿？

我想买一本关于中国青年的书。

我想买鲁迅的作品。

有这本书吗？

能试一下吗？

有大号的吗？

有镜子吗？

有小一点的吗？

我喜欢颜色鲜艳一点的。

我穿 42 号。

这条长裤不合我身。

腰部松了一些。

我可以看其他不同颜色的吗？

这件毛衣洗了会不会缩水？

我想买架全自动照相机。

我想买两个彩卷。

36 张的

mǎnǎo 玛瑙

Agate. The second most valuable, it is semi-transparent. Most agate pieces are red, white, or the two colors mixed.

xiù yù 岫玉 (and others)

Manchurian jasper. A serpentine, this stone is used in the less expensive jade pieces. This third category also includes other materials, such as crystals.

How to Bargain

You're at a free market. You see the perfect cotton vest to bring home for a souvenir. But the vendor is sharp – you know he's out to scalp you. How do you bring the price down? It takes creative thinking and determination. (B is the buyer, and V is the vendor).

B: *Zhèi jiàn mián bèixīn duōshao qián?*
How much is this cotton vest?

V: *Shí kuài qián.*
Ten yuan.

B: *Shénme! Kāi Wánxiào. Shí kuài qián! Tài guì le! Wǔ kuài zěnmeyàng?*
What? You've got to be kidding. Ten yuan! Too much! How's five yuan?

V: *Bù xíng, bù xíng. Gěi jiǔ kuài qián ba.*
No way, no way. Give me nine, then.

B: *Jiǔ kuài! Bú yào. Nǐ zhèi jiàn bèixīn zhìliàng bù hǎo. Zuìduō gěi nǐ qī kuài.*
Nine yuan! I don't want it. The quality of this vest is not very good. The most I'll offer is seven yuan.

V: *Qī kuài! Zài jiā yìdiǎn ba.*
Seven yuan! Come on, raise it a little.

B: *Hǎo le, hǎo le. Gěi nǐ qī kuài wǔ ba.*
Okay, okay. I'll give you seven and a half.

continued

SHOPPING

(135)mm	(yāo sān wǔ) de
(100)ASA	(yìbǎi) dù de
I'd like (Kodak) film.	Wǒ xiǎng yào (Kēdá) jiāojuǎn.
Where can I have (slides) processed?	Nǎr néng chōng (fǎnzhuǎn piàn)?
I'd like to have this film (developed).	Wǒ yào (chōng) jiāojuǎn.
Please do not (make prints).	Bú yào (kuòyìn).
I'd like to (order reprints).	Wǒ xiǎng (jiāyìn jǐ zhāng).
Please print (one) of this.	Zhèige qǐng yìn (yì) zhāng.
Please use (Fuji) paper.	Qǐng yòng (Fùshì) xiàngzhǐ.
When can I pick them up?	Shénme shíhou qǔ?
Can it be done earlier?	Néng zǎo yìdiǎn ma?
I'll be leaving town in (two) days.	(Liǎng) tiān hòu wǒ jiù zǒu le.

Returns and Repairs

I'd like to return this.	Wǒ xiǎng tuì huò.
It doesn't work.	Tā huài le.
Do you fix (cameras)?	Nǐmen xiū (zhàoxiàngjī) ma?
Something is wrong with the (shutter).	(Kuàimén) huài le.
Will you be able to fix it?	Néng xiū ma?
When will it be fixed?	Shénme shíhou néng xiū hǎo?

78

135 的

100 度的

我想要柯达胶卷。

哪儿能冲反转片？

我要冲胶卷。

不要扩印。

我想加印几张。

这个请印一张。

请用富士相纸。

什么时候取？

能早一点吗？

两天后我就走了。

我想退货。

它坏了。

你们修照相机吗？

快门坏了。

能修吗？

什么时候能修好？

V: Xíng. Mài gěi nǐ suàn le.
All right. I might as well sell it to you.

Renminbi

China's legal tender is Renminbi (RMB). Foreign currencies can not be used directly in China, though some shops illegally accept foreign currencies.

Foreign currencies may be converted into RMB at all banks, bank branches or hotels at the exchange rate quoted on the foreign exchange market on the day.

Black market in foreign currency is forbidden in China. People may approach you in front of hotels, at tourist spots or at banks for a black market exchange. You should be extremely careful. The exchange rate may be attractive—higher than the bank rate—but it is illegal and you risk being cheated.

What You'll Hear

bú mài	not for sale
Duōdà de?	How large?
huài le	broken
Jǐ hào de?	What size?
jiāoqián	pay
mài wán le	sold out
méi huò	out of stock
Nín yào shénme?	May I help you?
shōukuǎnchù	cashier's booth
yàngpǐn	sample
Zhǐ yǒu zhè yí gè.	It's the only one left.

Signs

bǎihuò shāngdiàn
Department Store

gōngyì měishù shāngdiàn
Arts and Crafts Store

dà jiǎnjià
Reduced Prices

shōu kuǎn tái
Cashier's Booth

yíngyè shíjiān
Business Hours

Entertainment

九
jiǔ 9

Zài lái yí gè!
Encore!

While in China, you can enjoy various kinds of evening entertainment. Most cities will have a few cultural performances going on each night, with the major cities offering many. The possibilities range from theater to song and dance, acrobatics, traditional Chinese music, and local opera. Occasionally you might even luck in on a special event, such as a sports competition or circus. If you feel ambitious, there's always the local cinema.

ENTERTAINMENT

Choosing a Show

I'd like to see a (play).	*Wǒ xiǎng kàn (huàjù).*
I'm very interested in (local opera).	*Wǒ duì (dìfāng xì) hěn gǎnxìngqù.*
Is the (performer) famous in China?	*Nèi wèi (yǎnyuán) zài Zhōngguó yǒumíng ma?*
When does the (concert) begin?	*(Yīnyuèhuì) shénme shíhou kāishǐ?*
May I bring a (tape recorder)?	*Wǒ néng dài (lùyīnjī) ma?*
When will the (show) be over?	*(Jiémù) shénme shíhou jiéshù?*
May we leave at (intermission)?	*Wǒmen néng zài (mùjiān xiūxi shí) líkāi ma?*
What (movie) is showing today?	*Jīntiān yǎn shénme (diànyǐng)?*
Is it in English?	*Shì Yīngwén duìbái ma?*
Are there English subtitles?	*Yǒu Yīngwén zìmù ma?*

Buying Tickets

I'd like (two) tickets for [tomorrow].	*Wǒ yào mǎi (liàng) zhāng [míngtiān] de piào.*
In the (front section), please.	*Qǐng gěi wǒ (qiánpái) de.*

Getting Seated

Excuse me, where are these seats?	*Duìbuqǐ, wǒmen de zuòwèi zài nǎr?*
What are your seat numbers?	*Nǐmen de zuòwèi hào shì duōshao?*
I believe those are our seats.	*Zhè shì wǒmen de zuòwèi.*
Is anyone sitting there?	*Nàr yǒu rén ma?*

我想看话剧。

我对地方戏很感兴趣。

那位演员在中国有名吗？

音乐会什么时候开始？

我能带录音机吗？

节目什么时候结束？

我们能在幕间休息时离开吗？

今天演什么电影？

是英文对白吗？

有英文字幕吗？

我要买两张明天的票。

请给我前排的。

对不起，我们的座位在哪儿？

你们的座位号是多少？

这是我们的座位。

那儿有人吗？

Musical Instruments

China's musical instruments have a long history. Some of them, such as the *sè* and the **shēng**, date from at least the Warring States Period (475-221 BC). When you go to a concert of traditional Chinese music, you can look for these instruments.

笛子	*dízi*	8-stop bamboo flute
二胡	*èrhú*	2-stringed fiddle, with lower register
古琴	*gǔqín*	7-stringed zither
京胡	*jīnghú*	2-stringed fiddle, with higher register
琵琶	*pípa*	4-stringed lute
三弦	*sānxián*	3-stringed guitar
瑟	*sè*	25-stringed zither
笙	*shēng*	Chinese mouth organ
唢呐	*suǒnà*	Chinese cornet (woodwind)
箫	*xiāo*	vertical bamboo flute
洋琴	*yángqín*	dulcimer
月琴	*yuèqín*	4-stringed round mandolin
筝	*zhēng*	many-stringed zither

Chinese Operas

There are many local Chinese operas, each with its own colorful style of music, dance, and costume. The six major ones are described below.

Peking Opera: Developed in the mid-nineteenth century when Peking was the capital of the Qing dynasty, this opera's lively repertoire includes many stories about political and military struggles.

continued

ENTERTAINMENT

There is someone here already.	*Zhèr yǐjīng yǒu rén le.*
Where can I get a (program)?	*Nǎr yǒu (jiémùdān)?*

Asking for Background

Who is (the director)?	*(Dǎoyǎn) shì shéi?*
Who plays (the Emperor)?	*Shéi yǎn (huángdì).*
What is the name of this (song-and-dance troupe)?	*Zhè shì něige (gēwǔtuán)?*
(Where) was the film shot?	*Zhè bù diànyǐng zài (nǎr) pāi de?*
(When) does the story take place?	*Zhè gùshi fāshēng zài (shénme shíjiān)?*
What (region) is this dance from?	*Zhè shì shénme (dìfāng) de wǔdǎo?*
How old are those (acrobats)?	*Zhèxiē (zájì yǎnyuán) duōdà le?*
How long have they (trained)?	*Tāmen (xùnliàn) le duōcháng shíjiān?*
Which (team) is that?	*Nà shì něige (duì)?*
What's the score?	*Bǐfēn shì duōshao?*

Showing Appreciation

This (music) is great.	*Zhè (yīnyuè) zhēn bàng!*
Where can I get a (tape) of it?	*Nǎr mài zhèige (lùyīndài)?*
The (show) was outstanding.	*Zhège (jiémù) hěn chūsè.*
It's been a really (pleasant) evening.	*Jīnwǎn guò de zhēn (yúkuài).*
I enjoyed it very much.	*Wǒ fēicháng xǐhuan.*

这儿已经有人了。

哪儿有节目单？

导演是谁？

谁演皇帝？

这是哪个歌舞团？

这部电影在哪儿拍的？

这故事发生在什么时间？

这是什么地方的舞蹈？

这些杂技演员多大了？

他们训练了多长时间？

那是哪个队？

比分是多少？

这音乐真棒！

哪儿卖这个录音带？

这个节目很出色。

今晚过得真愉快。

我非常喜欢。

Pingju Opera: Popular in northeastern areas such as Beijing, Tianjin, and Hebei, this is a lively and easy-to-understand folk opera.

Henan Opera: The rustic tunes of this opera are popular in Henan, Shaanxi, Shanxi, Hebei, Shandong, and Anhui Provinces.

Kunshan Opera: With clear singing and gentle gestures, this is one of the oldest traditional operas in China. It originated in the Kunshan area of Jiangsu Prov-ince.

Shaoxing Opera: The lyrical tunes of this opera originated from the folk songs of Shengxian County in Zhejiang Prov-ince.

Cantonese Opera: This opera has rich musical instrumentation and is popular in Guangdong, Guangxi, Taiwan, Hong Kong, and Macao.

What You'll Hear

guānzhòng	audience
Hǎo!	Bravo!
Hǎo qiú!	Good shot! (sports)
Jiāyóu!	Faster! Go! (sports)
nǚshìmen, xiānshengmen	ladies and gentlemen
Qǐng suí wǒ lái.	Please follow me.
xiūxi（shí） fēnzhōng	(ten)-minute intermission
Yǎnchū dào cǐ jiéshù.	The performance is now over.
Yǎnchū xiànzài kāishǐ.	The performance shall now begin.
Zài lái yí gè!	Encore!

Signs

shànglóu
Upstairs

xiàlóu
Downstairs

dānhào
Odd Numbers

shuānghào
Even Numbers

kèmǎn
Sold Out

+ shí 10 Health

Wǒ tóuténg.
I've got a headache.

Hopefully you will never have to use this chapter, but... if you ever do feel under the weather, the best thing to do is to take care of the illness quickly. Large hotels usually have a clinic or doctor's office for just that purpose. Once there, you will first be asked your name, age, nationality, and cities recently visited. Then it will be time to describe your complaints. The doctor may only know a few medical terms in English, so bear in mind the phrases here.

HEALTH

Getting Help

I need to (see a dentist).	*Wǒ yào (kàn yá).*
Where is the (clinic)?	*(Yīwùsuǒ) zài nǎr?*
Please take me to the (hospital).	*Qǐng dài wǒ qù (yīyuàn).*
Could you call an ambulance for me right away?	*Nǐ néng tì wǒ mǎshàng jiào jiùhùchē ma?*
When does the (clinic) open?	*(Yīwùsuǒ) shénme shíhou kāimén?*
Do they understand English?	*Tāmen dǒng yīngwén ma?*

Complaints

It hurts when I (talk).	*Yī (shuōhuà) jiù téng.*
It hurts here.	*Zhèr téng.*
I don't feel well.	*Wǒ juéde bù shūfu.*
I feel (faint).	*Wǒ (tóuyūn)*
I have a cold.	*Wǒ gǎnmào le.*
My arm is broken.	*Wǒ de shǒubì duàn le.*
My back went out.	*Wǒ niǔ dào yāo le.*
I'm allergic to (penicillin).	*Wǒ duì (qīngméisù) guòmǐn.*
I have (diabetes).	*Wǒ yǒu (tángniàobìng).*
I have (a cardiac condition).	*Wǒ yǒu (xīnzàngbìng).*
I'm pregnant.	*Wǒ huáiyùn le.*

Requests

Please take my (temperature).	*Qǐng tì wǒ liáng yíxià (tǐwēn).*

我要看牙。

医务所在哪儿？

请带我去医院。

你能替我马上叫救护车吗？

医务所什么时候开门？

他们懂英文吗？

一说话就疼。

这儿疼。

我觉得不舒服。

我头晕。

我感冒了。

我的手臂断了。

我扭到腰了。

我对青霉素过敏。

我有糖尿病。

我有心脏病。

我怀孕了。

请替我量一下体温。

Where Does It Hurt?

When telling the doctor where you have pain, the best method is to point to the afflicted area. You can also try using the Chinese words below.

ankle: **jiǎowàn**   脚腕
back: **bèibù**   背部
bone: **gútou**   骨头
ear: **ěrduo**   耳朵
eye: **yǎnjīng**   眼睛
hand: **shǒu**   手
head: **tóu**   头
heart: **xīnzàng**   心脏
hip: **kuà**   胯
joint: **guānjié**   关节
knee: **xīgài**   膝盖
leg: **tuǐ**   腿
muscle: **jīròu**   肌肉
neck: **bózi**   脖子
shoulder: **jiānbǎng**   肩膀
stomach: **wèi**   胃
throat: **hóulóng**   喉咙
tooth: **yáchǐ**   牙齿

Doctor, I Have...

Many of the common ailments of China travelers are due to the change of environment plus the fatigue of being on the road. The doctor will prescribe either traditional herbal medicines (quite effective) or Western pharmaceuticals. Here's how to describe your symptoms:

I have...
   Wǒ   我...
a cold
   gǎnmào le   感冒了

continued

89

HEALTH

Please give me some (medicine).	*Qǐng gěi wǒ diǎn (yào).*
I need some (aspirin).	*Wǒ yào diǎn (āsīpǐlín).*
Will you fill this prescription, please.	*Qǐng pèi zhèzhāng chǔfāng de yào.*

Questions

Is it (a contagious disease)?	*Shì (chuánrǎnbìng) ma?*
Can I (travel) tomorrow?	*Míngtiān wǒ néng (qù lǚxíng) ma?*
How long will this (illness) last?	*Zhèige (bìng) shénme shíhou néng hǎo?*
How should this medicine be taken?	*Zhèige yào zěnme chī fǎ?*
Should I take all this medicine?	*Zhèxiē yào dōu chī le ma?*
Take one pill three times a day after meals.	*Yìtiān sān cì, měicì yìlì, fàn hòu fúyòng.*
Do I need to come back for another session?	*Wǒ hái yào zài lái kàn ma?*

Taking Leave

You should have a thorought check-up.	*Nǐ yīnggāi hǎohǎo de jiǎnchá yíxià.*
I still feel rather weak.	*Wǒ gǎnjué háihěn xūruò.*
I feel much better now.	*Wǒ gǎnjué hǎo duō le.*
Thank you, doctor.	*Xièxie nín, dàifu.*

请给我点药。

我要点阿斯匹林。

请配这张处方的
药。

是传染病吗?

明天我能去旅行
吗?

这个病什么时候
能好?

这个药怎么吃法?

这些药都吃了吗?

一天三次,每次一
粒,饭后服用。

我还要再来看吗?

你应该好好地检
查一下。

我感觉还很虚弱。

我感觉好多了。

谢谢您,大夫。

constipation		
	yǒu diǎn biànmì	有点便秘
a cough		
	yǒu diǎn késou	有点咳嗽
diarrhea		
	lā dùzi	拉肚子
a fever		
	fāshāo	发烧
a headache		
	tóuténg	头疼
indigestion		
	xiāohuà bù liáng	消化不良
an infection		
	fāyán le	发炎了
insomnia		
	shīmián	失眠
nasal congestion		
	bízi bù tōng qì	鼻子不通气
a sore throat		
	hóulóng tòng	喉咙痛
a sprained ankle		
	jiǎowàn niǔ le	脚腕扭了

What You'll Hear

dǎzhēn	injection
jiā zài yèxià	put under your arm
liáng tǐwēn	take a temperature
měicì chī...	each time take...
Nǎli bù shūfu?	Where is the discomfort?
pào zài rèshuǐ lǐ	steep in hot water
tǎng xià	lie down
xiūxi	rest
yàofāng	prescription
yì tiān chī (sān) cì	take it (three) times a day

Signs

rénmín yīyuàn
People's Hospital

guàhào chù
Registration Office

ménzhěnbù
Outpatient Department

jízhěnshì
Emergency Room

yàofáng
Pharmacy

English-Chinese Dictionary

This is a simplified dictionary for the China traveler. The Chinese expressions here are colloquial equivalents, not academic translations, of the English entries. Where an entry has several meanings, a charification of the intended meaning appears in parentheses. Abbreviations used are: noun (n), verb (v), and adjective (adj). Be aware that some Chinese expressions cannot be used syntactically like the corresponding English. However, they can be used effectively as replacements within the sentence patterns of the text.

a, an	yī, yígè	一，一个
a few	jǐgè	几个
a little	yìdiǎn	一点
a while	yìhuǐr	一会儿
about(approximately)	dàyuē	大约
about(concerning)	guānyú	关于
above	zài... zhī shàng	在......之上
accept	jiēshòu	接受
accident	shìgù, yìwài	事故，意外
accompaniment (music)	bànzòu	伴奏
accompany	péi	陪
accordion	shǒufēngqín	手风琴
accurate	zhèngquè, zhǔnquè	正确，准确
achievement	chéngjì, chéngguǒ	成绩，成果
acre	yīngmǔ	英亩
acrid	sè	涩
acrobat	zájì yǎnyuán	杂技演员
acrobatics	zájì	杂技
acrylic(fiber)	bǐnglún	丙纶
acting(performance)	biǎoyǎn	表演
action	xíngdòng, dòngzuò	行动，动作
activity	huódòng	活动
actor(actress)	yǎnyuán	演员
acupressure	diǎnxuè fǎ	点穴法
acupuncture	zhēnjiǔ	针灸

DICTIONARY

acupuncture anesthesia	*zhēncì mázuì*	针刺麻醉
acute	*jíxìng*	急性
adaptor(outlet board)	*jiēxiànbǎn*	接线板
adaptor(outlet cube)	*sāntōng*	三通
adaptor plug	*zhuǎnjiē chātóu*	转接插头
add	*jiā*	加
address(n)	*dìzhǐ*	地址
addressee	*shōujiàn rén , duìfāng*	收件人,对方
adhesive plaster	*xiàngpí gāo*	橡皮膏
adjust	*tiáo*	调
adjustment	*tiáozhěng*	调整
administrator	*guǎnlǐ zhě*	管理者
adore	*rè'ài*	热爱
adult	*chéngrén , dàrén*	成人,大人
advanced	*xiānjìn*	先进
advertisement manager	*guǎnggào jīnglǐ*	广告经理
aerobics	*jiànměi cāo*	健美操
affair(matter)	*shìqing*	事情
afraid	*pà*	怕
Africa	*Fēizhōu*	非洲
after meals	*fànhòu*	饭后
afternoon	*xiàwǔ*	下午
again	*zài*	再
agate	*mǎnǎo*	玛瑙
age(of a person)	*niánlíng*	年龄
agriculture	*nóngyè*	农业
AIDS	*àizī bìng*	艾滋病
air	*kōngqì*	空气
air conditioner	*kōngtiáojī*	空调机
air conditioning	*kōngtiáo*	空调
air force	*kōngjūn*	空军
air pump	*qìbèng , qìtǒng*	气泵,气筒
air sick	*yūnjī*	晕机
air valve	*qìfá , qìmén*	气阀,气门
airline	*hángkōng gōngsī*	航空公司
airmail	*hángkōng yóujiàn*	航空邮件
airplane	*fēijī*	飞机
airport	*fēijīchǎng*	飞机场
airport departure tax	*jīchǎng fèi*	机场费

aisle	guòdào	过道
alarm clock	nàozhōng	闹钟
alcohol(fluid)	jiǔjīng	酒精
alcohol(liquor)	jiǔ	酒
alike	yíyàng , xiàng	一样,像
all	quánbù , dōu	全部,都
allergic	guòmǐn	过敏
allergy	guòmǐn zhèng	过敏症
alley	hútong	胡同
allspice	làméi	腊梅
almond	xìngrén	杏仁
almond-flour tea	xìngrénchá	杏仁茶
almond gelatin	xìngrén dòufu	杏仁豆腐
alone	dāndú	单独
already	yǐjīng	已经
also	yě	也
altitude	hǎibá	海拔
altogether	yígòng	一共
always	zǒngshì , lǎoshì	总是,老是
ambulance	jiùhùchē	救护车
analyze	fēnxī	分析
ancient	gǔdài	古代
and	hé , gēn	和,跟
anemia	pínxuě zhèng	贫血症
anesthesia	mázuì	麻醉
anesthetist	mázuì shī	麻醉师
angina pectoris	xīn jiǎotòng	心绞痛
angry	shēngqì	生气
animal	dòngwù	动物
ankle	jiǎowàn	脚腕
anniversary	zhōunián	周年
another	lìng yí yè , biéde	另一个,别的
answer(phone)	jiē	接...
answer(reply)	huídá	回答
ant	mǎyǐ	蚂蚁
antenna (for TV, radio)	tiānxiàn	天线
anthropology	rénlèixué	人类学
antibiotic	kàngshēngsù	抗生素
antipyretic	tuìshāo	退烧
antique	gǔdǒng	古董
antiseptic cream	xiāodú gāo	消毒膏

DICTIONARY

anxious	zhāojí	着急
any	rènhé	任何
apartment	dānyuán fáng , gōngyù	单元房,公寓
appetite	wèikǒu	胃口
applause	gǔzhǎng	鼓掌
apple	píngguǒ	苹果
apply for	shēnqǐng	申请
appreciate	xīnshǎng	欣赏
apprentice	xuétú	学徒
appropriate	héshì	合适
apricot	xìng	杏
April	sìyuè	四月
archaeology	kǎogǔ	考古
architecture	jiànzhù	建筑
area(measure)	miǎnjī	面积
area(realm)	lǐngyù , fànwéi	领域,范围
area(region)	dìqū	地区
argali sheep	tānyáng	滩羊
arm	gēbo , shǒubì	胳膊,手臂
armband	bìzhāng	臂章
armpit	yè	腋
army	bùduì , jūnduì	部队,军队
around (approximately)	zuǒyòu	左右
arrange	ānpái	安排
arrangement	ānpái	安排
arrive	dàodá	到达
art	yìshù	艺术
art director	yìshù zhǐdǎo	艺术指导
art exhibition	měishù zhǎnlǎn	美术展览
art gallery	huàláng	画廊
art museum	měishùguǎn	美术馆
art work	yìshùpǐn	艺术品
arthritis	guānjiéyán	关节炎
article(object)	wùpǐn	物品
arts and crafts	gōngyì měishù	工艺美术
arts and crafts store	gōngyì měishù shāngdiàn	工艺美术商店
ashtray	yānhuīgāng	烟灰缸
Asia	Yàzhōu	亚洲
ask	wèn	问
asparagus lettuce	wōsǔn	莴笋
aspen tree	báiyángshù	白杨树

aspirin	āsīpǐlín	阿斯匹林
assistant(n)	zhùshǒu , zhùlǐ	助手,助理
assistant manager (hotel)	dàtáng jīnglǐ	大堂经理
assorted	jīngxuǎn	精选
assorted cold dishes	lěng pīnpán	冷拼盘
asthma	qìchuǎn	气喘
at	zài	在
athlete	yùndòngyuán	运动员
Atlantic Ocean	Dàxīyáng	大西洋
atomic	yuánzǐ	原子
attend class	shàngkè	上课
attend school	shàngxué	上学
attention	zhùyì	注意
audience	guānzhòng	观众
auditorium	lǐtáng	礼堂
August	bāyuè	八月
aunt(see Appendix H)	āyí	阿姨
Australia	Àodàlìyà	澳大利亚
Australian dollar	àoyuán	澳元
author	zuòzhě	作者
automatic	zìdòng	自动
autumn	qiūtiān	秋天
avenue	dàjiē	大街
awhile	yìhuǐr	一会儿
azalea	dùjuānhuā	杜鹃花
back(direction)	hòu	后
back(n)	bèi	背
back door	hòumén	后门
back section(seating)	hòupái	后排
backpack	shuāngjiān kuàbāo	双肩挎包
backstage	hòutái	后台
backyard	hòuyuàn	后院
bad	huài	坏
badminton	yǔmáoqiú	羽毛球
bag	dài , dàizi	袋,袋子
baggage	xíngli	行李
baggage cart	xíngli chē	行李车
baggage claim area	xíngli tīng	行李厅
baggage claim office	xíngli bàngōng shì	行李办公室
baggage strap	xíngli dài	行李带

DICTIONARY

English	Pinyin	Chinese
baggage tag	*xíngli pái*	行李牌
balcony(seating)	*lóushàng zuòwei*	楼上座位
balcony(terrace)	*yángtái*	阳台
Bali	*Bālí*	巴厘
ball	*qiú*	球
ball game	*qiúsài*	球赛
ballet	*bāléiwǔ*	芭蕾舞
ballpoint pen	*yuánzhūbǐ*	圆珠笔
ballroom	*wǔtīng*	舞厅
bamboo	*zhúzi*	竹子
bamboo shoot	*zhúsǔn*	竹笋
bambooware	*zhúbiān*	竹编
banana	*xiāngjiāo*	香蕉
band(music group)	*yuèduì*	乐队
band(radio)	*bōduàn*	波段
Band-Aid	*chuāngkětiē*	创可贴
bandage(n)	*bēngdài*	绷带
Bangkok	*Màngǔ*	曼谷
bank(financial)	*yínháng*	银行
banquet	*yànhuì*	宴会
banquet manager	*yànhuìtīng jīnglǐ*	宴会厅经理
banyan tree	*róngshù*	榕树
bar(for drinks)	*jiǔbā*	酒吧
barber shop	*lǐfà diàn*	理发店
bargain prices	*yìjià*	议价
barley	*dàmài , qīngkē*	大麦,青稞
baseball	*bàngqiú*	棒球
basin(land)	*péndì*	盆地
basketball	*lánqiú*	篮球
bat	*biānfú*	蝙蝠
bath towel	*yùjīn*	浴巾
bathhouse	*zǎotáng*	澡堂
bathroom(for baths)	*yùshì*	浴室
bathroom(toilet)	*cèsuǒ*	厕所
bathtub	*yùchí*	浴池
batik	*làrǎn*	蜡染
battery	*diànchí*	电池
bayberry, red	*yángméi*	杨梅
be	*shì*	是
bean	*dòuzi*	豆子
bean paste	*dòushā*	豆沙
bean sauce, hot	*dòubàn jiàng*	豆瓣酱

bean sprout	dòuyá	豆芽
beancurd	dòufu	豆腐
bear(n)	xióng , gǒuxióng	熊,狗熊
beautiful	měilì , piàoliang	美丽,漂亮
beauty salon	fàláng	发廊
beaver	hǎilí	海狸
because	yīnwéi	因为
bed	chuáng	床
bedroom	wòshì	卧室
bedtime	shuìjiào shíjiān	睡觉时间
beef	niúròu	牛肉
beefsteak	niúpái	牛排
beer	píjiǔ	啤酒
beet	tiáncài	甜菜
before	yǐqián	以前
before meals	fànqián	饭前
before sleep	shuìqián	睡前
beggar	qǐgài	乞丐
begin	kāishǐ	开始
begonia	qiūhǎitáng	秋海棠
Beijing Opera	jīngjù	京剧
Belgium	Bǐlìshí	比利时
believe(faith)	xiāngxìn	相信
believe(opinion)	rènwéi	认为
bell(ancient)	gǔzhōng	古钟
bell captain	xíngli lǐngbān	行李领班
bell tower	zhōnglóu	钟楼
belong to	shǔyú	属于
below	zài . . . xiàmiàn	在……下面
Berlin	Bólín	柏林
berth	chuángwèi	床位
best	zuìhǎo	最好
better	gènghǎo	更好
bicycle	zìxíngchē	自行车
big	dà	大
bill(money notes)	piàozi	票子
bill(payment due)	zhàngdān	帐单
billiards	táiqiú	台球
billion	shíyì	十亿
biology	shēngwùxué	生物学
bird	niǎo	鸟
birthday	shēngrì	生日

DICTIONARY

biscuit	*bǐnggān*	饼干
bite(v)	*yǎo*	咬
bitter	*kǔ*	苦
bitter gourd	*kǔguā*	苦瓜
black	*hēi*	黑
black mushroom	*xiānggū , dōnggū*	香菇,冬菇
black tea	*hóngchá*	红茶
black-and-white	*hēibái*	黑白
blackboard	*hēibǎn*	黑板
bland	*dàn*	淡
blank tape	*kòngbái dài*	空白带
blanket(n)	*tǎnzi*	毯子
bleed	*liúxuè*	流血
blister	*pào*	疱
blocked(stopped up)	*dǔsè*	堵塞
blonde	*jīnfà*	金发
blood	*xuèyè*	血液
blood pressure	*xuèyā*	血压
blood type	*xuèxíng*	血型
blouse	*nǚ chènshān*	女衬衫
blow dry	*chuīgān*	吹干
blow dryer	*chuīfēngjī*	吹风机
blue	*lán*	蓝
blunt(dull)	*dùn*	钝
board game	*qísài*	棋赛
boarding pass	*dēngjī pái*	登机牌
boat	*chuán , zhōu*	船,舟
boat ride	*chéngchuán*	乘船
body(human)	*shēntǐ*	身体
boil(v)	*shāokāi , zhǔ*	烧开,煮
boiled dumplings	*shuǐjiǎo*	水饺
boiled egg	*zhǔ jīdàn*	煮鸡蛋
boiled water	*kāishuǐ*	开水
bok choy	*báicài*	白菜
bon voyage	*yílù shùnfēng*	一路顺风
bone	*gǔtou*	骨头
Bonn	*Bō'ēn*	波恩
bonsai	*pénjǐng*	盆景
bonus	*jiǎngjīn*	奖金
book(n)	*shū*	书
booking office	*dìngpiào chù*	订票处
bookkeeper	*kuàijì*	会计

bookstore	*shūdiàn*	书店
boring	*kūzào*	枯燥
borrow	*jiè*	借
Boston	*Bōshìdùn*	波士顿
bottle(n)	*píngzi*	瓶子
bottle opener	*pínggài qǐzi*	瓶盖起子
bourgeois	*zīchǎn jiējí*	资产阶级
bowel movement	*dàbiàn*	大便
bowels	*chángzi*	肠子
bowl(n)	*wǎn*	碗
bowling	*bǎolíng qiú*	保龄球
bowling alley	*bǎolíng qiúchǎng*	保龄球场
box(carton)	*hézi*	盒子
box office	*shòupiàochù*	售票处
boxing	*quánjī*	拳击
boy	*nánhái*	男孩
boyfriend	*nán péngyǒu*	男朋友
bracelet	*shǒuzhuó*	手镯
brakes	*zhá , sāchē*	闸,刹车
brandy	*báilándì*	白兰地
brass instrument	*tóngguǎn yuèqì*	铜管乐器
Bravo!	*Hǎo!*	好!
bread	*miànbāo*	面包
breakdancing	*pīlì wǔ*	霹雳舞
breakfast	*zǎofàn*	早饭
breathe	*hūxī*	呼吸
brick	*zhuāntou*	砖头
brick tea	*zhuānchá*	砖茶
bridge(n)	*qiáo*	桥
bright	*liàng , xiānyàn*	亮,鲜艳
brightness	*liàngdù*	亮度
bring	*dài , ná*	带,拿
Britain	*Yīngguó*	英国
broad bean	*cándòu*	蚕豆
broadcasting station	*guǎngbō diàntái*	广播电台
brocade	*zhījǐn*	织锦
broccoli, Chinese	*gàilán*	芥蓝
broken(out of order)	*huài le*	坏了
broken(severed)	*duàn le*	断了
bronchitis	*zhī qìguǎn yán*	支气管炎
bronze chariot	*tóng zhànchē*	铜战车
broom	*tiáozhou*	笤帚

DICTIONARY

broth	qīngtāng	清汤
brother(older)	gēge	哥哥
brother(younger)	dìdi	弟弟
brown	zōngsè	棕色
brown paper	niúpí zhǐ	牛皮纸
brown sauce	hóngshāo	红烧
(braised in)		
brush	shuāzi	刷子
Brussels	Bùlǔsài'ěr	布鲁塞尔
bubble gum	pàopaotáng	泡泡糖
buddha	fó	佛
buddhism	fójiào	佛教
building(n)	lóufáng, jiànzhù	楼房,建筑
bull	gōngniú	公牛
Bund(Shanghai)	Wàitān	外滩
bureau(organization)	jú	局
bureau director	júzhǎng	局长
burial grounds	mùdì	墓地
Burma	Miǎndiàn	缅甸
burn(n)	shāoshāng	烧伤
bus(n)	qìchē	汽车
bus driver	sījī	司机
bus map	qìchē xiànlù tú	汽车线路图
bus station	qìchē zǒngzhàn	汽车总站
bus stop	qìchē zhàn	汽车站
bushel	pǔshì'ěr	蒲式耳
business	shēngyì	生意
business	qǐyè guǎnlǐ	企业管理
management		
business person	shāngrén	商人
busy	máng	忙
busy line(phone)	zhànxiàn	占线
but	dànshì	但是
butcher shop	ròudiàn	肉店
butter	huángyóu	黄油
buttocks	pìgu	屁股
button(for clothing)	kòuzi	扣子
button(pushbutton)	ànniǔ	按纽
buy	mǎi	买
CAAC	Zhōngguó mínháng	中国民航
cabbage	yáng báicài	洋白菜

cabbage heart	càixīn	菜心
cabbage, Chinese	dà báicài	大白菜
cabin(ship)	cāng, chuáncāng	舱,船舱
cable address	diànbào guàhào	电报挂号
cable TV	bìlù diànshì	闭路电视
cadre	gànbù	干部
cadre's jacket	zhōngshān zhuāng	中山装
cafe	kāfēiguǎn	咖啡馆
cake	dàngāo	蛋糕
calendar	rìlì	日历
California	Jiāzhōu	加洲
call(to beckon)	jiào	叫
call(to telephone)	gěi...dǎdiànhuà	给……打电话
calligrapher	shūfǎjiā	书法家
calligraphy	shūfǎ	书法
calligraphy brush	máobǐ	毛笔
camel	luòtuo	骆驼
camelia	cháhuā	茶花
camera	zhàoxiàngjī	照像机
camphor tree	zhāngshù	樟树
can(know how to)	huì	会
can(possible to)	néng	能
can(tin, jar)	guàntou	罐头
can opener	guàntou qǐzi	罐头起子
Canada	Jiānádà	加拿大
canal	yùnhé	运河
cancel	qǔxiāo	取消
cancer	áizhèng	癌症
candied haws	bīngtáng húlu	冰糖葫芦
candy	táng, tángguǒ	糖,糖果
canoe	dúmùzhōu	独木舟
Canon	Jiā néng	佳能
Cantonese Opera	yuèjù	粤剧
capital(city)	shǒudū	首都
capital(money)	zījīn, zīběn	资金,资本
capitalist(n)	zīběnjiā	资本家
capon	yānjī	阉鸡
capsule	jiāonáng	胶囊
caption	zìmù	字幕
car	qìchē, xiǎojiàochē	汽车,小轿车
car sick	yùnchē	晕车
cardiac failure	xīnlì shuāijié	心力衰竭

DICTIONARY

cardiology	*xīnzàng bìngxué*	心脏病学
cards(playing)	*púkè pái*	扑克牌
career	*shìyè*	事业
careful	*xiǎoxīn*	小心
careless	*mǎdàhā*	马大哈
carpenter	*mùjiàng*	木匠
carpet	*dìtǎn*	地毯
carrot	*húluóbo*	胡萝卜
carry	*xiédài*	携带
carry-on luggage	*shǒutí xíngli*	手提行李
cart(n)	*tuīchē*	推车
cartoon(film)	*dònghuà piān*	动画片
cartoon(print)	*mànhuà*	漫画
carving(n)	*diāokè*	雕刻
cash(n)	*xiànjīn*	现金
cash(v)	*duìhuàn*	兑换
cash advance	*xiànjīn yùfù*	现金预付
cashew nut	*yāoguǒ*	腰果
cashier	*chū nà yuán*	出纳员
cashier's booth	*shōukuǎnchù*	收款处
cashmere	*kāishìmǐ*	开士米
casserole	*shāguō*	沙锅
cassette(sound tape)	*cídài*	磁带
cassia	*guìhuā*	桂花
cassia wine	*guìhuā jiǔ*	桂花酒
casual	*suíbiàn*	随便
cat	*māo*	猫
catch(v)	*zhuāzhù*	抓住
cathartic	*xièyào*	泻药
cattle	*shēngkou*	牲口
cauliflower	*càihuā*	菜花
cave	*shāndòng*	山洞
CCTV English Service	*diànshì yīngyǔ jiému*	电视英语节目
ceiling	*tiānhuābǎn*	天花板
celery	*qíncài*	芹菜
cellophane tape	*tòumíng jiāodài*	透明胶带
cement(concrete)	*shuǐní*	水泥
center(middle)	*zhōngjiān*	中间
cetigrade	*shèshì*	摄氏
centimeter	*límǐ*	厘米
Central America	*Zhōngměizhōu*	中美洲

century	shìjì	世纪
ceramics	táocí	陶瓷
certain	yídìng	一定
certificate	zhèngmíng	证明
chain	liàntiáo, liànzi	链条,链子
chair(n)	yǐzi	椅子
chairman	zhǔxí	主席
Chairman Mao	Máo zhǔxí	毛主席
chamber music	shìnèi yuè	室内乐
champagne	xiāngbīnjiǔ	香槟酒
champion	guànjūn	冠军
chance(opportunity)	jīhuì	机会
change (coins, small bills)	língqián	零钱
change(to replace, exchange)	huàn	换
change(transfer)	diào	调
change (transformation)	biànhuà	变化
channel(TV)	píndào	频道
character(role)	juésè	角色
characteristic	tèdiǎn	特点
charcoal drawing	tànhuà	炭画
charged'affaires	lǐngshì	领事
charming	mírén	迷人
cheap	piányi	便宜
cheapest	zuìpiányi	最便宜
check, bank	zhīpiào	支票
check in(for flight)	bàn chéngjī shǒuxù	办乘机手续
check in(register)	dēngjì	登记
check out(from a hotel)	tuìfáng	退房
checkers, Chinese	tiàoqí	跳棋
Cheers!	Gānbēi!	干杯!
cheese	nǎilào	奶酪
chef	chúshī	厨师
chemical(adj)	huàxué	化学
chemist's(drugstore)	yàodiàn	药店
chemistry	huàxué	化学
chemotherapy	huàliáo	化疗
cheongsam(gown)	qípáo	旗袍
cherry	yīngtáo	樱桃

DICTIONARY

chess	*guójì xiàngqí*	国际象棋
chess, Chinese	*xiàngqí*	象棋
chest pain	*xiōngkǒu tòng*	胸口痛
chestnut	*lìzi*	栗子
chewing gum	*kǒuxiāngtáng*	口香糖
Chicago	*Zhījiāgē*	芝加哥
chicken	*jī*	鸡
child	*xiǎohái*	小孩
children's clothing	*tóngzhuāng*	童装
children's palace	*shàonián gōng*	少年宫
chilli pepper(dried)	*gān làjiāo*	干辣椒
China	*Zhōngguó*	中国
China Central Television(CCTV)	*Zhōngyāng diànshì tái*	中央电视台
Chinese(language)	*Hànyǔ*	汉语
Chinese character	*Hànzì*	汉字
Chinese meal	*zhōngcān*	中餐
Chinese menu	*zhōngcān càipǔ*	中餐菜谱
Chinese New Year	*chūnjié*	春节
chives, Chinese	*jiǔcài*	韭菜
chocolate	*qiǎokèlì*	巧克力
choice	*xuǎnzé*	选择
cholera	*huòluàn*	霍乱
choose	*xuǎn, tiāo*	选, 挑
chop(seal)	*yìnzhāng shí, túzhāng*	印章石, 图章
chopsticks	*kuàizi*	筷子
chorus	*kéchàng*	合唱
Christmas	*Shèngdànjié*	圣诞节
chronic	*mànxìng*	慢性
chrysanthemum	*júhuā*	菊花
chrysolite(jade)	*fěicuì*	翡翠
church	*jiàotáng*	教堂
cigarette	*xiāngyān*	香烟
cinema	*diànyǐng yuàn*	电影院
circle(n)	*quān*	圈
circus	*mǎxì*	马戏
citizen	*gōngmín*	公民
city	*chéngshì*	城市
city gate	*chéngmén*	城门
city map	*chéngshì jiāotōng tú*	城市交通图
city tour	*yóulǎn shìróng*	游览市容
civil	*mínyòng*	民用

clams	géli	蛤蜊
clap(applaud)	gǔzhǎng	鼓掌
class(social)	jiējí	阶级
class(students)	bān	班
classic	gǔdiǎn	古典
classroom	jiàoshì , kètáng	教室,课堂
clay	niántǔ	粘土
clay figure	nírén	泥人
clean(adj)	gānjìng	干净
clean(v)	dǎsǎo	打扫
cleaning solution	xiāodú yè	消毒液
clear(distinct)	qīngchǔ	清楚
climb	pá	爬
clinic	wèishēngsuǒ	卫生所
clock	zhōng	钟
cloisonne	jǐngtàilán	景泰蓝
cloisonne vase	jǐngtàilán huāpíng	景泰蓝花瓶
close(to shut)	guān	关
closed(business)	guānmén	关门
closed(not public)	bù kāifàng	不开放
closet	yīguì	衣柜
cloth	bù , liàozi	布,料子
clothespin	yīfujiā	衣服夹
clothing	yīfu	衣服
clothing store	fúzhuāng diàn	服装店
cloud	yún	云
cloudyweather	yīn , duōyún	阴,多云
club(recreation)	jùlèbù	俱乐部
coach(sports)	jiàoliàn	教练
coal	méi	煤
coat	shàngyī , dàyī	上衣,大衣
coat hanger	yījià	衣架
Coca-Cola	Kěkǒu Kělè	可口可乐
cocaine	kěkǎyīn	可卡因
cock's comb(flower)	jīguānhuā	鸡冠花
cockroach	zhāngláng	蟑螂
cocoa	kōukou	可可
coconut	yēzi	椰子
cocoon	cánjiǎn	蚕茧
coffee	kāfēi	咖啡
coffee shop	kāfēi diàn	咖啡店
cola	kělè	可乐

cold(adj)	lěng	冷
cold(illness)	gǎnmào, zháoliáng	感冒,着凉
cold drink	lěngyǐn	冷饮
cold drinking water	liángbáikāi	凉白开
cold milk	lěng niúnǎi	冷牛奶
cold platter	lěngpán	冷盘
cold water(from tap)	lěngshuǐ	冷水
cold-water wash	lěngshuǐ xǐ	冷水洗
cold wave(perm)	lěngtàng	冷烫
collect(gather)	shōují	收集
collect(phone call)	duìfāng fùkuǎn	对方付款
college	xuéyuàn, dàxué	学院,大学
color(n)	yánsè	颜色
color TV	cǎidiàn	彩电
colored	cǎisè	彩色
column(pillar)	zhùzi	柱子
coma	hūnmí	昏迷
comb(n)	shūzi	梳子
come	lái	来
comedy	xǐjù	喜剧
comfortable	shūfu	舒服
commemorative stamp	jìniàn yóupiào	纪念邮票
common	pǔtōng	普通
commune	gōngshè	公社
communist party	gòngchǎndǎng	共产党
compact disc	jīguāng chàngpiàn	激光唱片
company(business)	gōngsī	公司
company account	gōngsī zhànghù	公司帐户
complain	bàoyuàn	抱怨
completely	wánquán	完全
composer(music)	zuòqǔjiā	作曲家
composition(music)	zuòpǐn	作品
composition (painting)	gòutú	构图
comprehensive	zōnghé	综合
computer	jìsuànjī, diànnǎo	计算机,电脑
computer programmer	diànnǎo chéngxùyuán	电脑程序员
comrade	tóngzhì	同志
concerning	guānyú	关于
concert	yīnyuèhuì	音乐会

concert hall	*yīnyuè tīng*	音乐厅
concierge (hotel)	*jiēdàiyuán*	接待员
concubine	*fēizi , qiè*	妃子,妾
condition	*tiáojiàn , qíngkuàng*	条件,情况
conditioner (for hair)	*hùfàsù*	护发素
conductor (bus)	*shòupiàoyuán*	售票员
conductor (music)	*zhǐhuī*	指挥
conductor (train)	*chéngwùyuán*	乘务员
conference room	*huìyìshì*	会议室
confirm	*quèdìng*	确定
connect	*jiē*	接
connecting flight	*xiánjiē hángbān*	衔接航班
connection (relation)	*guānxi*	关系
conscience	*liángxīn*	良心
consider	*kǎolǜ*	考虑
consomme	*qīngtāng*	清汤
constipation	*biànmì*	便秘
Constitution	*xiànfǎ*	宪法
construction	*jiànshè*	建设
contact lens	*yǐnxíng yǎnjìng*	隐形眼镜
contact prints (photo)	*xiǎoyàng*	小样
contagious	*jiēchù chuánrǎn*	接触传染
container	*róngqì*	容器
contemporary (adj)	*dāngdài*	当代
continent	*dàlù*	大陆
contraceptives	*bìyùn yòngpǐn*	避孕用品
contrast (n)	*duìbǐ*	对比
convenient	*fāngbiàn*	方便
convulsion	*jìngluán*	痉挛
cook (n)	*chúshī, dà shīfu*	厨师,大师傅
cook (prepare meals)	*zuòfàn*	做饭
cookie	*bǐnggān*	饼干
cooking	*pēngtiáo*	烹调
cool (adj)	*liáng , liángkuài*	凉,凉快
copy (n)	*fùběn*	副本
corduroy	*dēngxīn róng*	灯芯绒
coriander	*xiāngcài*	香菜
cork carving	*ruǎnmù diāo*	软木雕
corkscrew	*píngsāi qǐzi*	瓶塞起子
corn	*yùmǐ*	玉米
cornet, Chinese	*suǒnà*	锁呐
corporation	*gōngsī*	公司

DICTIONARY

correct(yes)	duì	对
costume	xìzhuāng	戏装
cot	zhédié chuáng	折叠床
cottage(thatched)	cǎofáng	草房
cotton	mián	棉
cotton-padded jacket	miányī	棉衣
cotton-padded shoes	miánxié	棉鞋
cough	késòu	咳嗽
cough drops	hánpiàn	含片
cough syrup	zhǐké tángjiāng	止咳糖浆
country(nation)	guójiā	国家
country(rural)	xiāngcūn	乡村
country music	xiāngcūn yīnyuè	乡村音乐
countryside	nóngcūn	农村
county	xiàn	县
countyard	yuànzi	院子
cover(n)	gàizi	盖子
cow	nǎiniú	奶牛
crab	pángxiè	螃蟹
crabapple, Chinese	hǎitáng	海棠
craft	gōngyì	工艺
craftsman	gōngjiàng	工匠
cramp	chōujīn	抽筋
crane	hè	鹤
crayons	làbǐ	蜡笔
cream(dairy)	nǎiyóu	奶油
creator	chuàngzào zhě	创造者
credit card	xìnyòngkǎ	信用卡
crepe(pancake)	jiānbǐng	煎饼
crispy	cuì	脆
crispy duck	xiāngsū yā	香酥鸭
critical condition	qíngkuàng wēijí	情况危急
crop(n)	nóngzuòwù	农作物
cross(pass)	guò	过
cross talk(comedy routine)	xiàngsheng	相声
crosswalk	rénxíng héngdào	人行横道
cruise(v)	yóu	游
cruise boat	yóutǐng	游艇
cry(sob)	kū	哭
cub	yòuzǎi	幼仔
cucumber	huángguā	黄瓜

cultural exchange	wénhuà jiāoliú	文化交流
cultural relic	wénhuà gǔjì	文化古迹
Cultural Revolution	wéngé	文革
culture (arts, customs)	wénhuà	文化
cup	bēi, bēizi	杯,杯子
curler(for hair)	fàjuǎn	发卷
curling iron	měifà qì	美发器
curly	juǎnqū shì	卷曲式
curry	gālí	咖喱
curtain(theater)	mù	幕
curtain(window)	chuānglián	窗帘
cushion	diànzi	垫子
custom(tradition)	fēngsú	风俗
custom-made	dìngzuò de	订做的
customer	gùkè	顾客
Customs	hǎiguān	海关
customs declaration	hǎiguān shēnbào dān	海关申报单
customs duty	guānshuì	关税
cut(v)	jiǎn, qiē	剪,切
cuttlefish	mòdǒuyú, wūzéi	墨斗鱼,乌贼
cycling	qí zìxíngchē	骑自行车
cymbals	chǎ	镲
cypress tree	bǎishù	柏树
daily(newspaper)	rìbào	日报
Dalai Lama	Dálài Lǎma	达赖喇嘛
dam	dībà	堤坝
damaged	nònghuài le	弄坏了
damp	shī	湿
dance(n)	wǔdǎo	舞蹈
dance(v)	tiàowǔ	跳舞
dance drama	wǔjù	舞剧
dance hall	wǔtīng	舞厅
dance party	wǔhuì	舞会
dance troupe	wǔdǎo tuán	舞蹈团
dancer	wǔdǎo yǎnyuán	舞蹈演员
danger	wēixiǎn	危险
dark	hēi	黑
darkroom	ànshì	暗室
date(appointment)	yuēhuì	约会
date(fruit)	zǎo	枣

DICTIONARY

dating(courtship)	*tán liàn'ài*	谈恋爱
daughter	*nǚér*	女儿
day	*rì , tiān*	日,天
day after tomorrow	*hòutiān*	后天
day-lily bud	*jīnzhēn*	金针
daytime	*báitiān*	白天
deaf	*lóng*	聋
December	*shí'èryuè*	十二月
decide	*juédìng*	决定
declare(at Customs)	*shēnbào*	申报
decongestant	*bítōng*	鼻通
decoration	*zhuāngshì*	装饰
deep	*shēn*	深
deep-fried	*zhá*	炸
deer	*lù*	鹿
degree(temperature)	*dù*	度
delicatessen	*shúshí diàn*	熟食店
delicious	*hǎochī*	好吃
democracy	*mínzhǔ*	民主
demonstration (in street)	*yóuxíng*	游行
Denmark	*Dānmài*	丹麦
dentist	*yákē yīshēng*	牙科医生
dentist's office	*yákē zhěnsuǒ*	牙科诊所
depart	*líkāi*	离开
department	*bùmén , kē*	部门,科
department store	*bǎihuò shāngdiàn*	百货商店
departure time (planes)	*qǐfēi shíjiān*	起飞时间
deposit(bank)	*chǔxù*	储蓄
deposit(pledge)	*yājīn*	押金
depressed(mood)	*qíngxù bù hǎo*	情绪不好
dermatologist	*pífūkē yīshēng*	皮肤科医生
dermatology department	*pífūkē*	皮肤科
descend	*xià*	下
descend(planes)	*jiàngluò*	降落
describe	*xíngróng*	形容
desert	*shāmò*	沙漠
design(v)	*shèjì*	设计
designer	*shèjìshī*	设计师

designer (name brand)	míngpái	名牌
desk	shūzhuō	书桌
dessert	diǎnxin	点心
detergent	qùwūfěn	去污粉
detour	wānlù	弯路
develop(film)	chōng, chōngxǐ	冲,冲洗
diabetes	tángniàobìng	糖尿病
diagnosis	zhěnduàn	诊断
dial(v)	bō	拨
dialog(theater)	duìbái	对白
diamond	zuànshí	钻石
diaphragm(camera)	guāngquān	光圈
diarrhea	lā dùzi	拉肚子
diced meat or vegetable	dīng	丁
die(v)	sǐ, qùshì	死,去世
diet(foods eaten)	yǐnshí	饮食
diet(weight loss)	jiéshí	节食
dietician	yíngyǎng yīshī	营养医师
different	bù yíyàng	不一样
difficulty	kùnnán	困难
dig	wā	挖
dignified	yǒu qìpài	有气派
diligent	qínfèn	勤奋
dim sum	diǎnxin	点心
dining car	cānchē	餐车
dining room	cāntīng	餐厅
dinner(supper)	wǎnfàn	晚饭
dip(v)	zhàn	蘸
diplomat	wàijiāoguān	外交官
diplomatic	wàijiāo	外交
director(artistic)	dǎoyǎn	导演
director(of an organization)	zhǔrèn	主任
dirty	zāng	脏
disastrous	zāogāo	糟糕
disco	dísīkē	迪斯科
discomfort	bù shūfu	不舒服
discount(n)	zhékòu	折扣
discover	fāxiàn	发现
discussion	tǎolùn	讨论

DICTIONARY

dish(plate, tray)	*pán*	盘
dishwashing liquid	*xǐdíjì*	洗涤剂
disinfectant	*xiāodújì*	消毒剂
disk film	*pán shì jiāopiàn*	盘式胶片
disperse	*sàn*	散
distance	*jùlí*	距离
district	*qū*	区
disturb	*dǎrǎo, gānrǎo*	打扰,干扰
divide	*fēn*	分
divorce	*líhūn*	离婚
dizzy	*tóuyūn*	头晕
do(be occupied with)	*zuò*	做
do business	*zuò shēngyì*	做生意
Do not...	*bié, búyào...*	别,不要……
dock(n)	*mǎtóu*	码头
doctor	*yīshēng, dàifu*	医生,大夫
documentary(film)	*jìlù piān*	记录片
doesn't work	*bù xíng*	不行
dog	*gǒu*	狗
dollar	*yuán*	元
domestic(national)	*guónèi*	国内
don't mind(object to)	*bú zàihu*	不在乎
Donald Duck	*Tánglǎoyā*	唐老鸭
door	*mén*	门
door god	*ménshén*	门神
dormitory	*sùshè*	宿舍
double(adj)	*shuāng*	双
double bed	*shuāngrén chuáng*	双人床
double happiness	*shuāngxǐ*	囍
double-sided embroidery	*shuāngmiàn xiù*	双面锈
dough figure	*miànrén*	面人
down	*xià*	下
downstairs	*lóuxià*	楼下
downtown	*shìzhōngxīn*	市中心
dragon	*lóng*	龙
Dragon Well tea	*Lóngjǐng chá*	龙井茶
dragon dance	*lóngwǔ*	龙舞
drain(n)	*xiàshuǐdào*	下水道
drama	*xìjù*	戏剧
drawing	*túhuà*	图画
dress rehearsal	*cǎipái*	彩排

dresser	yīchú	衣橱
dressing room	huàzhuāng shì	化装室
dried bean curd	dòufu gān	豆腐干
dried shrimps	hǎimǐ	海米
drink	hē	喝
drive(v)	kāichē	开车
driver (bus,taxi)	sījī	司机
driver's license	jiàshǐ zhízhào	驾驶执照
drop(n)	dī	滴
drop(v)	diào	掉
drug	yào	药
drug(narcotic)	dúpǐn	毒品
drugstore	yàodiàn	药店
drum(n)	gǔ	鼓
drum tower	gǔlóu	鼓楼
dry	gān	干
dry clean	gānxǐ	干洗
dry white wine	gān bái pútao jiǔ	干白葡萄酒
dubbed film	yìzhì piān	译制片
duck	yāzi	鸭子
duet(instrumental)	èrchóngzòu	二重奏
duet(vocal)	èrchóngchàng	二重唱
dulcimer	yángqín	扬琴
dull(uninteresting)	dāndiào, méi yìsi	单调,没意思
dumb(mute)	yǎ	哑
dumplings	jiǎozi, bāozi	饺子,包子
duplication machine	fùyìn jī	复印机
during	zài...zhōng	在……中
dustpan	bòji	簸箕
dusty	huīchén duō	灰尘多
dynasty	cháodài	朝代
dysentery	lìji	痢疾
each	měi, měigè	每,每个
each time	měicì	每次
ear	ěrduo	耳朵
ear-nose-throat specialist	ěr-bí-hóu kē dàifu	耳鼻喉科大夫
early	zǎo	早
earn	zhèng	挣
earth(planet)	dìqiú	地球
east	dōng	东

DICTIONARY

English	Pinyin	Chinese
East China Sea	*Dōnghǎi*	东海
easy	*róngyì*	容易
eat	*chī*	吃
Economic Daily	*Jīngjì Rìbào*	经济日报
economics	*jīngjìxué*	经济学
economy	*jīngjì*	经济
economy class	*pǔtōng cāngwèi*	普通舱位
edge	*biān*	边
editor	*biānjí*	编辑
education	*jiàoyù*	教育
eel	*shànyú*	鳝鱼
effect	*xiàoguǒ*	效果
efficiency	*xiàolǜ*	效率
egg	*jīdàn*	鸡蛋
egg-drop soup	*dànhuātāng*	蛋花汤
egg white	*dànbái , dànqīng*	蛋白,蛋清
eggplant	*qiézi*	茄子
Egypt	*Āijí*	埃及
eight	*bā*	八
eight precious rice	*bābǎofàn*	八宝饭
eighty	*bāshí*	八十
ejaculation	*shèjīng*	射精
elbow	*zhǒu*	肘
election	*xuǎnjǔ*	选举
electrical equipment	*diànqì*	电器
electricity	*diàn*	电
electronic	*diànzǐ*	电子
electrotherapy	*diànliáo*	电疗
elephant	*dàxiàng*	大象
elevator	*diàntī*	电梯
elm tree	*yúshù*	榆树
embarrassed	*bùhǎo yìsi*	不好意思
embassy	*dàshǐguǎn*	大使馆
embroidery	*cìxiù*	刺绣
emergency	*jǐnjí qíngkuàng*	紧急情况
emergency room	*jízhěn shì*	急诊室
emetic	*cuītùjì*	催吐剂
emperor	*huángdì*	皇帝
employee	*gùyuán*	雇员
empress	*huánghòu , nǚhuáng*	皇后,女皇
empress dowager	*tàihòu*	太后
empty(adj)	*kōng*	空

enamel	*tángcí*	搪瓷
encephalitis	*nǎoyán*	脑炎
Encore!	*Zài lái yí gè!*	再来一个!
end(v)	*jiéshù*	结束
energy(spirit)	*jīnglì*	精力
engine	*fādòngjī*	发动机
engineer	*gōngchéngshī*	工程师
England	*Yīngguó*	英国
English(language)	*Yīngyǔ*	英语
engraving	*diāokè*	雕刻
enjoy	*xǐhuan*	喜欢
enlargement	*fàngdà*	放大
enough	*zúgòu*	足够
ensemble (instrumental)	*hézòu*	合奏
enter	*jìn*	进
entrance	*rùkǒu , jìnkǒu*	入口 , 进口
entrepreneur	*qǐyè jiā*	企业家
entry visa	*rùjìng qiānzhèng*	入境签证
envelope	*xìnfēng*	信封
episode	*chāqǔ*	插曲
equal(adj)	*píngděng , yíyàng*	平等 , 一样
equal(v)	*děngyú*	等于
eraser	*xiàngpí*	橡皮
escalator	*zìdòng fútī*	自动扶梯
especially	*tèbié*	特别
et cetera	*děng*	等
eunuch	*tàijiān*	太监
Europe	*Ōuzhōu*	欧洲
even(more)	*gèng*	更
evening	*wǎnshang*	晚上
everyday	*měitiān*	每天
everyone	*dàjiā*	大家
everything	*yíqiè*	一切
everywhere	*dàochù*	到处
evil	*huài*	坏
example	*lìzi*	例子
exceed	*chāoguò*	超过
excellent	*fēicháng hǎo*	非常好
excellent(slang)	*bàng*	棒
exchange(ideas)	*jiāoliú*	交流
exchange(money)	*duìhuàn*	兑换

DICTIONARY

exchange rate	duìhuàn lǜ	兑换率
exciting	lìngrén jīdòng	令人激动
excuse me (make way)	láojia	劳驾
excuse me (pardon)	duìbuqǐ	对不起
exercise (physical)	duànliàn	锻炼
exhibition	zhǎnlǎn	展览
exit (n)	chūkǒu	出口
exit visa	chūjìng qiānzhèng	出境签证
expectation	qīwàng	期望
expense	fèiyòng	费用
expensive	guì	贵
experience (n)	jīngyàn	经验
experiment	shìyàn	试验
expert	zhuānjiā	专家
expertise	zhuāncháng	专长
explain	jiěshì	解释
export goods	chūkǒu huò	出口货
export license	chūkǒu xǔkě zhèng	出口许可证
express (speed)	tèkuài	特快
express (to convey)	biǎodá	表达
extension (phone)	fēnjī	分机
extension cord	diànxiàn	电线
external use	wàiyòng	外用
extra (surplus)	fùyù de	富余的
extra large	tèdà hào	特大号
extra small	tèxiǎo hào	特小号
extract a tooth	báyá	拔牙
extremely	jí	极
eye (n)	yǎnjīng	眼睛
eye drops	yǎn yàoshuǐ	眼药水
face (n)	liǎn	脸
face cream	miànshuāng	面霜
facial (n)	měiróng	美容
factory	gōngchǎng	工厂
Fahrenheit	huáshì	华氏
faint	tóuhūn	头昏
fake	màopái	冒牌
fall (v)	shuāidǎo, diào	摔倒, 掉
false	jiǎ de	假的
family	jiā, jiātíng	家, 家庭

family members	jiātíng chéngyuán	家庭成员
fan, electric	diànshàn	电扇
fan, folding	zhéshàn	折扇
fan, hand-held	shànzi	扇子
Fantastic!	Juéle!	绝了!
far	yuǎn	远
fare (bus, taxi, or train)	chēfèi	车费
farm	nóngchǎng	农场
farmer	nóngmín	农民
farmer's home	nóngjiā	农家
fast(speed)	kuài	快
fast food	kuàicān	快餐
fat(adj)	pàng	胖
fat(n)	zhīfáng	脂肪
father	fùqin	父亲
faucet	lóngtóu	龙头
feature film	gùshì piān	故事片
February	èryuè	二月
fee	fèi	费
feel(sense)	juéde	觉得
female(animals)	cí, mǔ	雌,母
female(people)	nǚ	女
fencing	jījiàn	击剑
fertilizer	féiliào	肥料
fever	fāshāo	发烧
few	hěnshǎo, bù duō	很少,不多
fiction	xiǎoshuō	小说
fiddle, Beijing opera	jīnghú	京胡
fiddle, two-stringed	èrhú	二胡
field(farm)	tián	田
field(for athletics)	yùndòng chǎng	运动场
fifty	wǔshí	五十
fig	wúhuāguǒ	无花果
fill a tooth	bǔyá	补牙
fill in (a form)	tián	填
film(for camera)	jiāojuǎn	胶卷
film(movie)	diànyǐng	电影
film festival	diànyǐng jié	电影节
film studio	diànyǐng chǎng	电影厂
final(adj)	zuìhòu	最后
finally	zhōngyú	终于

DICTIONARY

find(v)	zhǎo	找
fine(delicate)	jīngzhì	精致
fine(good)	hěnhǎo, tǐnghǎo	很好,挺好
fine arts	yìshù	艺术
finger	shǒuzhǐ	手指
fingernail polish	zhǐjiǎ yóu	指甲油
fingernail polish remover	tuìguāng shuǐ	退光水
finish(v)	wánchéng	完成
finished	wán le	完了
Finland	Fēnlán	芬兰
fire(n)	huǒ	火
fire equipment	mièhuǒ qì	灭火器
fire escape	ānquán tī	安全梯
fire exit	tàipíng mén	太平门
fire fighter	xiāofáng duìyuán	消防队员
first(beforehand)	xiān	先
first, the	dìyī	第一
first-aid station	jíjiù zhàn	急救站
first class(seat)	tóuděng cāng	头等舱
first run(bus or train)	shǒu bān chē, tóu bān chē	首班车,头班车
fish	yú	鱼
fisherfolk	yúmín	渔民
fishing	diàoyú	钓鱼
fishing village	yúcūn	渔村
five	wǔ	五
five-grain liquor	wǔliángyè	五粮液
fix(repair)	xiūlǐ	修理
flag(n)	qí	旗
flash(camera)	shǎnguāng dēng	闪光灯
flashlight	shǒudiàntǒng	手电筒
flask	hú	壶
flight(airline)	hángbān	航班
flight schedule	fēixáng shíkèbiǎo	飞行时刻表
floor(of a room)	dìbǎn	地板
floor(story)	céng, lóu	层,楼
flour	miànfěn	面粉
flower	huā	花
flu	liúgǎn	流感
fluent	liúlì	流利
flute, bamboo	dízi	笛子

fly(insect)	*cāngying*	苍蝇
fly(v)	*fēi*	飞
Flying Pigeon(bike)	*Fēigē*	飞鸽
fog	*wù*	雾
folder	*jiāzi*	夹子
folk dance	*mínjiān wǔdǎo*	民间舞蹈
folk music	*mínjiān yīnyuè*	民间音乐
folk tale	*mínjiān gùshì*	民间故事
folklore	*mínjiān chuánshuō*	民间传说
follow	*gēn*	跟
food	*shípǐn , shíwù*	食品,食物
food poisoning	*shíwù zhòng dú*	食物中毒
foot(12 inches)	*yīngchǐ*	英尺
foot(body)	*jiǎo , zú*	脚,足
football(American)	*gǎnlǎnqiú*	橄榄球
footlight	*jiǎodēng*	脚灯
for example	*bǐrú , bǐfang shuō*	比如,比方说
Forbidden City (Palace Museum)	*Gùgōng*	故宫
foreign	*wàiguó*	外国
foreign affairs office	*wàishì bàngōngshì*	外事办公室
foreign exchange certificate	*wàihuì*	外汇
foreign exchange desk	*wàibì duìhuàn tái*	外币兑换台
foreign expert	*wàiguó zhuānjiā*	外国专家
foreign guest	*wàibīn*	外宾
foreign policy	*wàijiāo zhèngcè*	外交政策
foreign student	*liúxuéshēng*	留学生
foreigner	*wàiguórén*	外国人
forest	*sēnlín*	森林
Forever(bike)	*Yǒngjiǔ*	永久
forget	*wàngjì*	忘记
forgive	*yuánliàng*	原谅
fork	*chāzi*	叉子
fork(road)	*chà lùkǒu*	叉路口
form(printed sheet)	*biǎogé*	表格
forty	*sìshí*	四十
forward(sports)	*qiánfēng*	前锋
four	*sì*	四
fox	*húlí*	狐狸
fracture	*gǔzhé*	骨折

DICTIONARY

fragile	*yìsuì*	易碎
fragrant	*xiāng*	香
franc	*fǎláng*	法郎
France	*Fǎguó*	法国
free(no charge)	*miǎnfèi*	免费
free market	*zìyóu shìchǎng*	自由市场
freedom	*zìyóu*	自由
freelancer	*zìyóu zhíyè zhě*	自由职业者
freeze	*dòng*	冻
freezing	*bīngdòng*	冰冻
fresh	*xīnxian*	新鲜
Friday	*xīngqī wǔ*	星期五
fried, deep	*zhá*	炸
fried, lightly	*jiān*	煎
fried crisp chicken	*xiāngsū jī*	香酥鸡
fried cruller	*yóutiáo*	油条
fried dumplings (pot-stickers)	*guōtiē*	锅贴
fried egg	*jiān jīdàn*	煎鸡蛋
fried noodles	*chǎomiàn*	炒面
fried rice	*chǎofàn*	炒饭
fried sesame twists	*máhuā*	麻花
friend	*péngyǒu*	朋友
friendship	*yǒuyì*	友谊
Friendship Store	*Yǒuyì Shāngdiàn*	友谊商店
fries, potato	*zhá tǔdòu*	炸土豆
frog	*qīngwā*	青蛙
front	*qián*	前
front door	*qiánmén*	前门
front section(seating)	*qiánpái*	前排
front yard	*qiányuàn*	前院
fruit	*shuǐguǒ*	水果
fuel	*ránliào*	燃料
Fuji	*Fùshì*	富士
full	*mǎn*	满
full(after meal)	*bǎo le*	饱了
fun	*yǒuqù, hǎowán*	有趣, 好玩
funny(amusing)	*kě xiào, dòu*	可笑, 逗
fur	*qiúpí, pímáo*	裘皮, 皮毛
furnace	*gāolú, lúzi*	高炉, 炉子
furniture	*jiājù*	家俱
fuse(n)	*bǎoxiǎnsī*	保险丝

gallon	*jiālún*	加仑
game	*yóuxì*	游戏
game room	*yóuyì shì*	游艺室
garbage can	*lājī xiāng*	垃圾箱
garden	*huāyuán*	花园
garlic	*suàn*	蒜
gas(coal)	*méiqì*	煤气
gas(vapor)	*qì , qìtǐ*	气,气体
gas station	*jiāyóu zhàn*	加油站
gas stove	*méiqìlú*	煤气炉
gas tank	*yóuxiāng*	油箱
gasoline	*qìyóu*	汽油
gastric	*wèi*	胃
gastric perforation	*wèi chuānkǒng*	胃穿孔
gastritis	*wèiyán*	胃炎
gate	*mén*	门
gear(driving)	*dǎng*	档
gear(part)	*chǐlún*	齿轮
general anesthesia	*quánshēn mázuì*	全身麻醉
Geneva	*Rìnèiwǎ*	日内瓦
geranium	*xiùqiú*	绣球
Germany	*Déguó*	德国
gesture	*dòngzuò*	动作
get(obtain)	*dé*	得
get off(a vehicle)	*xiàchē*	下车
get off work	*xiàbān*	下班
get on(a vehicle)	*shàng chē*	上车
giant panda	*dàxióngmāo*	大熊猫
gift	*lǐwù*	礼物
gin(liquor)	*dùsōngzǐ jiǔ*	杜松子酒
ginger	*shēngjiāng*	生姜
ginkgo	*yínxìng , báiguǒ*	银杏,白果
ginkgo tree	*báiguǒ shù*	白果树
ginseng	*rénshēn*	人参
girl	*nǚhái*	女孩
girlfriend	*nǚ péngyǒu*	女朋友
give	*gěi*	给
give away	*sòngdiào*	送掉
give up hope	*xièqì*	泻气
glass(cup)	*bōli bēi*	玻璃杯
glasses(optical)	*yǎnjìng*	眼镜
glassware	*bōli zhìpǐn*	玻璃制品

DICTIONARY

glaucoma	qīngguāng yǎn	青光眼
glucose	pútáo táng	葡萄糖
glue(mucilage)	jiāoshuǐ	胶水
glue(paste)	jiànghu	浆糊
glutinous rice cake	niángāo	年糕
go(board game)	wéiqí	围棋
go(v)	qù	去
Go! (sports)	Jiā yóu!	加油!
go around (an obstacle)	ràokāi	绕开
goalie(sports)	shǒuményuán	守门员
goat	shānyáng	山羊
gold	jīn	金
golden-haired monkey	jīnsīhóu	金丝猴
goldfish	jīnyú	金鱼
golf	gāo'ěrfū	高尔夫
gong	luó	锣
good	hǎo	好
good luck	hǎo yùnqi	好运气
good morning	zǎochén hǎo	早晨好
good-bye	zàijiàn	再见
good-looking	hǎokàn	好看
goods(stock)	huò	货
goose	é	鹅
gorge	xiá	峡
government	zhèngfǔ	政府
grade school	xiǎoxué	小学
graduate(v)	bìyè	毕业
grain(crop)	liángshi	粮食
grain coupon	liángpiào	粮票
gram	kè	克
grammar	yǔfǎ	语法
Grand Canal	Dàyùnhé	大运河
granddaughter	sūnnǚ, wài sūnnǚ	孙女,外孙女
grandfather (maternal)	lǎoye, wàigōng	姥爷,外公
grandfather(paternal)	yéye	爷爷
grandmother (maternal)	lǎolao, wàipó	姥姥,外婆
grandmother (paternal)	nǎinai	奶奶

grandson	*sūnzi , wàisūn*	孙子,外孙
grape	*pútáo*	葡萄
grasp(v)	*zhuā*	抓
gray	*huīsè*	灰色
Great!	*Zhēn bàng!*	真棒!
Great Hall of the People	*Rénmín Dàhuìtáng*	人民大会堂
Great Wall	*Chángchéng*	长城
Greece	*Xīlà*	希腊
green	*lǜ*	绿
green onion	*dàcōng*	大葱
green tea	*lǜchá*	绿茶
greeting card	*jìniàn kǎ*	纪念卡
grilled	*kǎo*	烤
groceries	*shípǐn*	食品
grocery store	*shípǐn diàn*	食品店
grotto	*shíkū*	石窟
ground(n)	*dì*	地
ground meat	*ròumò*	肉末
group(people)	*tuántǐ , qún*	团体,群
group visa	*jítǐ qiānzhèng*	集体签证
grow(plant)	*zhòng*	种
guarantee	*bǎozhèng*	保证
guard(sports)	*hòuwèi*	后卫
guesthouse	*bīnguǎn , zhāodàisuǒ*	宾馆,招待所
guide(person)	*dǎoyóu*	导游
guidebook	*dǎoyóu shū*	导游书
guitar	*jíta*	吉他
guitar, 3-string	*sānxián qín*	三弦琴
gun	*qiāng*	枪
gymnasium	*tǐyùguǎn*	体育馆
gymnastics	*tǐcāo*	体操
gynecologist	*fùkē yīshēng*	妇科医生
gynecology department	*fùkē*	妇科
habit(custom)	*xíguàn*	习惯
hair	*tóufa*	头发
hair oil	*fàyóu*	发油
hairbrush	*tóushuā*	头刷
haircut	*lǐfà*	理发
hairspray	*dìngxíng yè*	定型液

DICTIONARY

half	yíbàn , bànge	一半,半个
half a day	bàntiān	半天
half-price	bànjià	半价
halt	zhànzhù	站住
ham	huǒtuǐ	火腿
hammer	chuízi	锤子
hand(n)	shǒu	手
hand carry-on	suíshēn xíngli	随身行李
hand towel	shǒujīn	手巾
hand wash	shǒu xǐ	手洗
handball	shǒuqíu	手球
handicapped person	cánjí rén	残疾人
handicraft	shǒugōngyì pǐn	手工艺品
handkerchief	shǒujuàn	手绢
handlebar(bike)	chēbǎ	车把
handmade	shǒugōng zhìzuò	手工制作
happen	fāshēng	发生
happiness	xìngfú	幸福
happiness(symbol)	xǐ	喜
harbor	gǎng	港
hard-seat	yìngzuò	硬座
hard-sleeper	yìngwò	硬卧
harvest(n)	shōuhuò	收获
hat	màozi	帽子
hate	hèn	恨
have	yǒu	有
haw	shānzhā	山楂
Hawaii	Xiàwēiyí	夏威夷
hay fever	huāfěn rè	花粉热
he	tā	他
head	tóu	头
headache	tóuténg	头疼
headlight	qiándēng	前灯
health	jiànkāng	健康
health care	bǎojiàn	保健
health club	jiànshēn fáng	健身房
health declaration	jiànkāng biǎo	健康表
heart	xīnzàng , xīn	心脏,心
heart attack	xīnzàngbìng fāzuò	心脏病发作
heat(energy)	rèliàng , rè	热量,热
heat(radiator)	nuǎnqì	暖气
heat(v)	jiārè	加热

heavy	chén , zhòng	沉，重
heavy(taste)	nóng	浓
hectare	gōngqīng	公顷
hedge rose	qiángwēi	蔷薇
height	gāodù	高度
hello	nǐhǎo	你好
help(n)	bāngzhù	帮助
help(v)	bāng	帮
Helsinki	Hè'ěrxīnjī	赫尔辛基
hemorrhage	chūxuè	出血
Henan Opera	yùjù	豫剧
hepatitis	gānyán	肝炎
her	tāde	她的
herbal medicine	cǎoyào	草药
here	zhèlì , zhèr	这里，这儿
hero	yīngxióng	英雄
heroin	hǎiluòyīn	海洛因
heroine	nǚ yīngxióng	女英雄
hesitation	yóuyù	犹豫
hey	wèi	喂
high	gāo	高
high school	zhōngxué	中学
highest	zuìgāo	最高
highland	gāoyuán	高原
highway	gōnglù	公路
hill	shān	山
Hilton	Xī'ěrdùn	希尔顿
Himalayas	Xǐmǎlāyǎ shān	喜玛拉雅山
hip	kuà	胯
hire(a person)	gù	雇
hire(charter)	bāo	包
hired car	bāochē	包车
his	tāde	他的
history	lìshǐ	历史
history museum	lìshǐ bówùguǎn	历史博物馆
hold(embrace)	bào	抱
hold(take)	ná	拿
holder	jiàzi	架子
holiday	jiérì	节日
Holland	Hélán	荷兰
Hollywood	Hǎoláiwū	好莱坞
home	jiā	家

DICTIONARY

home-style	*jiācháng*	家常
homemaker	*zhǔfù*	主妇
Honda	*Běntián*	本田
honey crystalized apples	*básī píngguǒ*	拔丝苹果
Hong Kong	*Xiānggǎng*	香港
Hong Kong dollar	*gǎngbì*	港币
honor	*róngxìng*	荣幸
hook(n)	*gōuzi*	钩子
hope	*xīwàng*	希望
horrible	*kěpà*	可怕
hors d'oeuvre	*lěngpán*	冷盘
horse	*mǎ*	马
hospital	*yīyuàn*	医院
hospitality	*hàokè , zhāodài*	好客,招待
host(person)	*zhǔrén*	主人
host organization	*jiēdài dānwèi*	接待单位
hostel	*lǚshè*	旅社
hot	*rè*	热
hot(spicy)	*là*	辣
hot-and-sour soup	*suānlà tāng*	酸辣汤
hot pot	*luǒguō*	火锅
hot sauce	*làjiàng*	辣酱
hot spring	*wēnquán*	温泉
hot water(from tap)	*rèshuǐ*	热水
hotel	*lǚguǎn , fàndiàn*	旅馆,饭店
hour	*xiǎoshí*	小时
house	*fángzi*	房子
housekeeping department	*kèfáng bù*	客房部
how	*zěnme*	怎么
how far	*duōyuǎn*	多远
how long(length)	*duōcháng*	多长
how long(time)	*duōjiǔ*	多久
how many	*jǐ gè , duōshao*	几个,多少
how much	*duōshao*	多少
how old(person)	*duōdà*	多大
humid	*cháoshī*	潮湿
humor	*yōumò*	幽默
humor, sense of	*yōumò gǎn*	幽默感
hundred	*bǎi*	百
hundred million	*yì*	亿

hunting	*dǎliè*	打猎
hurry up	*gǎnkuài*	赶快
hurt	*téng*	疼
husband	*zhàngfu , àirén*	丈夫,爱人
Hyatt	*Kǎiyuè*	凯乐
hypertension	*gāo xuèyā*	高血压
hypodermic	*píxià*	皮下
hypotension	*dī xuèyā*	低血压
I	*wǒ*	我
ice	*bīng*	冰
ice cream	*bīngqílín*	冰淇淋
ice hockey	*bīngqiú*	冰球
ice water	*bīngshuǐ*	冰水
idea	*zhúyì , xiǎngfǎ*	主意,想法
idiom	*chéngyǔ*	成语
if	*rúguǒ*	如果
illness	*bìng*	病
image	*xíngxiàng*	形象
imitate	*mófǎng*	模仿
immediately	*mǎshàng*	马上
immigrant	*yímín*	移民
immigration checkpoint	*yímín jiǎnchá zhàn*	移民检查站
implement(a policy)	*zhíxíng*	执行
import	*jìnkǒu*	进口
import goods	*jìnkǒu huò*	进口货
import license	*jìnkǒu xǔkězhèng*	进口许可证
important	*zhòngyào*	重要
impression(thought)	*yìnxiàng*	印象
inch(n)	*yīngcùn*	英寸
increase	*zēngjiā*	增加
India	*Yìndù*	印度
indigestion	*xiāohuà bù liáng*	消化不良
indvidual	*gèrén , gètǐ*	个人,个体
industry	*gōngyè , chǎnyè*	工业,产业
inexpensive	*búguì*	不贵
infection	*fāyán*	发炎
infectious	*chuánrǎn*	传染
inflammation	*fāyán*	发炎
information (knowledge)	*zhīshi*	知识

129

DICTIONARY

information(news)	xiāoxi	消息
information desk	wènxùn chù	问询处
injection	zhùshè , dǎzhēn	注射,打针
ink(for calligraphy)	mòzhī	墨汁
ink(for fountain pen)	mòshuǐ	墨水
ink painting, Chinese	shuǐmò huà	水墨画
ink slab	yàntai	砚台
ink stick	mò	墨
Inner Mongolia	Nèiměnggǔ	内蒙古
inpatient department	zhùyuàn chù	住院处
inquire	xúnwèn	询问
insect	kūnchóng	昆虫
inside	lǐ	里
insignia(badge)	huīzhāng	徽章
insomnia	shīmián	失眠
instrumental music	qìyuè	器乐
insure	bǎoxiǎn	保险
intellectual	zhīshi fènzǐ	知识分子
intelligent	cōngming	聪明
interesting	yǒu yìsi	有意思
intermission	mùjiān xiūxi	幕间休息
intern	shíxí shēng	实习生
internal	nèi	内
international	guójì	国际
interpreter	fānyì	翻译
intersection	shízì lùkǒu	十字路口
(crossroad)		
intravenous injection	jìngmài zhùshè	静脉注射
introduction	jièshào	介绍
inventor	fāmíngzhě	发明者
investigate	diàochá	调查
invitation card	qǐngtiě	请帖
iron(for clothing)	yùndǒu	熨斗
iron(metal)	tiě	铁
iron(v)	yùn , tàng	熨,烫
Iron Goddess of	Tiěguānyīn chá	铁观音茶
Mercy tea		
iron openwork	tiěhuā	铁花
is	shì	是
isolation ward	gélí bìngfáng	隔离病房
it	tā	它
It's a pity	hěn yíhàn	很遗憾

It's nothing	*méi guānxi*	没关系
Italian opera	*Yìdàlì gējù*	意大利歌剧
Italy	*Yìdàlì*	意大利
itch	*yǎng*	痒
itinerary	*rìchéng*	日程
ivory	*xiàngyá*	象牙
ivory carving	*yádiāo*	牙雕
jacket	*jiākè*	夹克
jade	*yù*	玉
jade carving	*yùdiāo*	玉雕
jade carving factory	*yùdiāo chǎng*	玉雕厂
jail	*jiānyù*	监狱
jam(jelly)	*guǒjiàng*	果酱
January	*yīyuè*	一月
Japan	*Rìběn*	日本
Japanese yen	*rìyuán*	日元
jar	*píng, guàn*	瓶,罐
jasmine tea	*mòlì huāchá*	茉莉花茶
jaw	*xiàba*	下巴
jaywalking	*luàn chuān mǎlù*	乱穿马路
jazz music	*juéshìyuè*	爵士乐
jeep	*jípǔchē*	吉普车
jellyfish	*hǎizhé*	海蜇
jetlag	*shíchā fǎnying*	时差反应
jewel(precious)	*zhūbǎo*	珠宝
jewelry(ornamental)	*shǒushì*	首饰
job	*gōngzuò*	工作
join	*cānjiā*	参加
joints(body)	*guānjié*	关节
joke(v)	*kāi wánxiào*	开玩笑
journal(diary)	*rìjì*	日记
journal(periodical)	*qīkān, kānwù*	期刊,刊物
journalism	*xīnwén gōngzuò*	新闻工作
journalist(reporter)	*jìzhě*	记者
judge(n)	*fǎguān*	法官
judge(v)	*pànduàn*	判断
judo	*róudào*	柔道
juice(fruit)	*guǒzhī*	果汁
July	*qīyuè*	七月
jump	*tiào, bèng*	跳、蹦
jumprope(n)	*tiàoshéng*	跳绳
June	*liùyuè*	六月

DICTIONARY

just	jiù	就
just now	cái, gāngcái	才,刚才
karst	yánróng	岩溶
Keemun tea	Qímén hóngchá	祁门红茶
keep	bǎoliú	保留
ketchup(catsup)	fānqié jiàng	蕃茄酱
key(n)	yàoshi	钥匙
keyboard instrument	jiànpán yuèqì	健盘乐器
kick(v)	tī	踢
kidney	shèn	肾
kidney bean	yúndòu	云豆
kidskin	xiǎoshānyáng pí	小山羊皮
Kiev	Jīfǔ	基辅
kill(v)	shā	杀
kilogram	gōngjīn	公斤
kilometer	gōnglǐ	公里
kind(personality)	shànliáng	善良
kindergarten	yòu'éryuán	幼儿园
kiss(n)	qīn, wěn	亲,吻
kitchen	chúfáng	厨房
kite	fēngzheng	风筝
knee	xīgài	膝盖
knife	dāozi	刀子
knit	zhī	织
know(a fact)	zhīdao	知道
know(a person)	rènshì	认识
know how to	huì	会
knowledge	zhīshi	知识
Kodak	Kēdá	柯达
Korea	Cháoxiǎn	朝鲜
Kowloon	Jiǔlóng	九龙
Kublai Khan	Hūbìliè	忽必烈
kumquat	jīnjú	金桔
Kunshan Opera	kūnqǔ	昆曲
Kyoto	jīngdū	京都
label(n)	biāoqiān	标签
labor union	gōnghuì	工会
laboratory	huàyàn shì	化验室
lacquer, carved	diāoqī	雕漆
lacquerware	qīqì	漆器
lake	hú	湖

lamasery	*lǎmasì*	喇嘛寺
lamb(mutton)	*yángròu*	羊肉
lambskin	*xiǎoyáng pí*	小羊皮
lamp	*dēng*	灯
land(earth)	*tǔdì*	土地
landscape	*fēngjǐng*	风景
lane	*hútong, xiàng*	胡同,巷
language	*yǔyán*	语言
large	*dà*	大
largest	*zuìdà*	最大
last(final)	*zuìhòu*	最后
last month	*shàng ge yuè*	上个月
last one	*zuìhòu yígè*	最后一个
last run(bus or train)	*mòbān chē*	末班车
last week	*shàng ge xīngqī*	上个星期
last year	*qùnián*	去年
later(afterwards)	*hòulái*	后来
later(in a while)	*yíhuìr*	一会儿
laundry(clean)	*xǐ wán de yīfu*	洗完的衣服
laundry(dirty)	*yào xǐ de yīfu*	要洗的衣服
laundry bag	*xǐyīdài*	洗衣袋
laundry detergent	*xǐyīfěn*	洗衣粉
law	*fǎlǜ*	法律
lawyer	*lǜshī*	律师
layered	*duōcéng*	多层
lazy	*lǎn*	懒
lead(v)	*dài, lǐng*	带,领
lead actor(or actress)	*zhǔyǎn*	主演
leader	*lǐngdǎo*	领导
leads to(street)	*tōngxiàng*	通向
leaf	*shùyè*	树叶
leak(v)	*lòu*	漏
lean(thin)	*shòu*	瘦
leapord	*bào*	豹
learn	*xué*	学
leather	*pígé*	皮革
leather shoes	*píxié*	皮鞋
leave(behind)	*liú*	留
leave(depart)	*líkāi*	离开
leave(set out)	*chūfā*	出发
leave a message (spoken)	*liú huà*	留话

DICTIONARY

leave a note	*liú tiáo*	留条
lecture(n)	*jiǎngzuò*	讲座
left(direction)	*zuǒ*	左
leg	*tuǐ*	腿
lemon	*níngméng*	柠檬
lemonade	*níngméng shuǐ*	柠檬水
length	*chángdù*	长度
Leningrad	*Shèngbǐdébǎo*	圣彼德堡
lens(camera)	*jìngtóu*	镜头
less	*shǎo*	少
lesser panda	*xiǎoxióngmāo*	小熊猫
lesson(class)	*kè*	课
lesson(moral)	*jiàoxùn*	教训
let	*ràng*	让
letter(mail)	*xìn*	信
lettuce	*wōjù*	莴苣
level(degree)	*shuǐpíng*	水平
Li River	*Líjiāng*	漓江
liberalism	*zìyóuhuà*	自由化
library	*túshūguǎn*	图书馆
license plate	*chēpái*	车牌
lie down	*tǎng xià*	躺下
life	*shēnghuó*	生活
light(in color, density)	*qiǎn, dàn*	浅,淡
light(lamp)	*dēng*	灯
light(to kindle)	*diǎn*	点
light(weight)	*qīng*	轻
light meter	*cèguāng biǎo*	测光表
lighting	*zhàomíng*	照明
lighting design	*dēngguāng shèjì*	灯光设计
like(v)	*xǐhuan*	喜欢
like this(this way)	*zhèyàng*	这样
lilac	*dīngxiāng*	丁香
line(n)	*xiàn*	线
linen	*yàmá bù*	亚麻布
linguistics	*yǔyánxué*	语言学
lion	*shīzi*	狮子
lion dance	*shīzi wǔ*	狮子舞
liquor	*jiǔ*	酒
lira	*lǐlā*	里拉
listen to	*tīng*	听

listen to music	tīng yīnyuè	听音乐
liter	shēng	升
literature	wénxué	文学
lithograph	shíbǎnhuà	石版画
little(small)	xiǎo	小
live(reside)	zhù	住
live telecast	xiànchǎng zhíbō	现场直播
liver	gān	肝
living	huózhe	活着
living room	kètīng	客厅
lobby(n)	xiūxishì	休息室
lobster	lóngxiā	龙虾
local(place)	dìfāng	地方
local(slow bus or train)	mànchē	慢车
local(within a city)	běndì, dāngdì	本地,当地
local anesthesia	júbù mázuì	局部麻醉
local guide	dìpéi	地陪
local money, Chinese	rénmínbì	人民币
local opera	dìfāng xì	地方戏
located at	zài	在
location	dìdiǎn	地点
lock	suǒ	锁
lock(ship)	chuánzhá	船闸
locust tree	huáishù	槐树
London	Lúndūn	伦敦
lonely	jìmò	寂寞
long(adj)	cháng	长
long bean, green	jiāngdòu	江豆
long-distance	chángtú	长途
long-distance bus	chángtú qìchē	长途汽车
long live...	...wànsuì	……万岁
longan fruit	lóngyǎn	龙眼
longevity	chángshòu	长寿
longevity(symbol)	shòu	寿
look	kàn	看
loose	sōngsǎn	松散
loquat	pípá	枇杷
Los Angeles	Luòshānjī	洛杉矶
lose	diūshī	丢失
lost(an object)	diū le	丢了
lost(the way)	mílù	迷路

DICTIONARY

lost-and-found office	*shīwù zhāolǐng chù*	失物领招处
lotus flower	*liánhuā , héhuā*	莲花,荷花
lotus root	*ǒu*	藕
lotus seed	*liánzǐ*	莲子
loud	*dàshēng*	大声
love(n)	*àiqíng*	爱情
love(v)	*ài*	爱
low	*dī*	低
lowest	*zuìdī*	最低
luck	*yùnqi*	运气
luck(symbol)	*fú*	福
luggage(see baggage)	*xíngli*	行李
luggage rack	*xíngli jià*	行李架
lumbago	*yāoténg*	腰疼
lunch(n)	*wǔfàn*	午饭
lung	*fèi*	肺
lute, 4-string	*pípá*	琵琶
lychee(litchi)	*lìzhī*	荔枝
lynx	*shēli*	猞猁
lyric(song)	*gēcí*	歌词
Macao	*Āomén*	澳门
machine	*jīqì*	机器
Madrid	*Mǎdélǐ*	马德里
magazine(reading)	*zázhì*	杂志
magic	*móshù*	魔术
magician	*móshùshī*	魔术师
mah-jongg	*májiàng*	麻将
mail(letters)	*xìn*	信
mail(v)	*jì*	寄
mailbox	*yóutǒng*	邮筒
main	*zhǔyào*	主要
main character	*zhǔjué*	主角
main desk	*zǒngtái*	总台
maitre d'	*zǒngguǎn*	总管
make	*zuò*	做
make progress	*yǒu jìnzhǎn*	有进展
make-up(cosmetics)	*huàzhuāng*	化妆
malaria	*nüèjí*	疟疾
male(animals)	*gōng , xióng*	公,雄
male(people)	*nán*	男

man	*nánrén*	男人
management	*guǎnlǐ*	管理
manager	*jīnglǐ*	经理
Manchurian jasper	*xiùyù*	岫玉
mandarin ducks	*yuānyang*	鸳鸯
mandarin orange	*gānzi*	柑子
mandolin, 4-string	*yuèqín*	月琴
mango	*mángguǒ*	芒果
manicure	*xiū zhǐjia*	修指甲
manual transmission (car)	*shǒudòng huàndǎng*	手动换档
manufacture (produce)	*shēngchǎn*	生产
many	*hǎo duō*	好多
Mao cap	*jūnmào*	军帽
Mao jacket	*jūnbiànfú*	军便服
Maotai liquor	*máotái*	茅台
map(n)	*dìtú*	地图
marble	*dàlǐshí*	大理石
March	*sānyuè*	三月
Marco Polo	*Mǎkě Bōluó*	马可·波罗
marijuana	*dàmá*	大麻
marine(military)	*hǎijūn lùzhànduì*	海军陆战队
marionette	*tíxiàn mù'ǒu*	提线木偶
mark(currency)	*mǎkè*	马克
marriage	*hūnyīn*	婚姻
marry	*jiéhūn*	结婚
marten	*diāo*	貂
martial arts	*wǔshù*	武术
martial arts performer	*wǔshù biǎoyǎnzhě*	武术表演者
martyr	*lièshì*	烈士
mashed potatos	*tǔdòu ní*	土豆泥
mask	*miànjù*	面具
massage	*ànmó, tuīná*	按摩,推拿
masses(people)	*qúnzhòng*	群众
master worker	*shīfu*	师傅
matches	*huǒchái*	火柴
maternity ward	*chǎnkē bìngfáng*	产科病房
mathematics	*shùxué*	数学
matter(affair)	*shìqing*	事情

DICTIONARY

mausoleum	*líng*	陵
Maxwell House	*Màishì*	麦氏
May	*wǔyuè*	五月
maybe	*yěxǔ*	也许
me	*wǒ*	我
meaning	*yìsi*	意思
measles	*mázhěn*	麻疹
measure(v)	*cèliáng*	测量
meatball	*ròu wánzi*	肉丸子
medical science	*yīxué*	医学
medicine	*yīyào*	医药
medicine, traditional Chinese	*zhōngyào*	中药
medium(size)	*zhōng hào*	中号
meet(a person)	*jiàn*	见
meeting(n)	*huì*	会
Melbourne	*Mò'ěrběn*	墨尔本
melon, Hami	*hāmìguā*	哈蜜瓜
member(of a group)	*chéngyuán*	成员
memorial arch	*páilou*	牌楼
memorial hall	*jìniàntáng*	纪念堂
memory	*jìyì*	记忆
men's bike	*nánchē*	男车
mend	*bǔ*	补
meningitis	*nǎomó yán*	脑膜炎
menstruation	*yuèjīng*	月经
mental	*jīngshén*	精神
menu	*càidān*	菜单
Mercedes Benz	*Bēnchí*	奔驰
merchandise	*shāngpǐn*	商品
metal	*jīnshǔ*	金属
meter(metric)	*mǐ*	米
meter(taxi)	*jìjiàqì*	计价器
method	*fāngfǎ*	方法
metric ton	*gōngdūn*	公吨
Mickey Mouse	*Mǐlǎoshǔ*	米老鼠
microphone	*huàtǒng*	话筒
midnight	*bànyè*	半夜
mile	*yīnglǐ*	英里
military	*jūnshì*	军事
military band	*jūnyuèduì*	军乐队

milk	*niúnǎi*	牛奶
Milky Way	*Yínhé*	银河
milliliter	*háoshēng*	毫升
millimeter	*háomǐ*	毫米
million	*bǎiwàn*	百万
mind (brain)	*tóunǎo*	头脑
mine (my)	*wǒde*	我的
mineral water	*kuàngquán shuǐ*	矿泉水
Ming Tombs	*Shísānlíng*	十三陵
mini-bus	*miànbāochē*	面包车
miniature bottle painting	*bíyānhú*	鼻烟壶
miniature carving	*wēidiāo*	微雕
mink	*shuǐdiāo*	水貂
Minolta	*Měinéngdá*	美能达
minorities' dance	*mínzú wǔdǎo*	民族舞蹈
minority nationality	*shǎoshù mínzú*	少数民族
minute (n)	*fēnzhōng*	分钟
mirror (n)	*jìngzi*	镜子
miscellaneous	*záwù, záshì*	杂务, 杂事
mischievous	*táoqì*	淘气
Miss	*xiǎojiě*	小姐
mistake (n)	*cuòwù*	错误
mistake (v)	*nòngcuò, gǎocuò*	弄错, 搞错
Mitsubishi	*Sānlíng*	三菱
model (of an object)	*móxíng*	模型
model (person)	*mótèr*	模特儿
modern (advanced)	*xiàndài*	现代
modern (style)	*xiàndàipài*	现代派
modernization	*xiàndàihuà*	现代化
monastery	*sì, sìyuàn*	寺, 寺院
Monday	*xīngqī yī*	星期一
money	*qián*	钱
money order	*huìpiào*	汇票
Mongolian hot pot	*shuànyángròu*	涮羊肉
monk	*héshàng*	和尚
monkey	*hóuzi*	猴子
monster	*móguǐ, guàiwù*	魔鬼, 怪物
month	*yuè*	月
monthly ticket (bus, subway)	*yuèpiào*	月票

DICTIONARY

monument	*jìniànbēi*	纪念碑
moon	*yuèliang, yuè*	月亮,月
mop (n)	*tuōbǎ*	拖把
mop (v)	*tuōdì*	拖地
more	*duō*	多
morning	*zǎochén, shàngwǔ*	早晨,上午
morphine	*mǎfēi*	吗啡
Moscow	*Mòsīkē*	莫斯科
Moslem	*qīngzhēn*	清真
mosque	*qīngzhēn sì*	清真寺
mosquito	*wénzi*	蚊子
most (comparative)	*zuì*	最
most (majority of)	*dà duōshù*	大多数
mother	*mǔqīn*	母亲
motor	*mǎdá*	马达
Mount Everest	*Zhūmùlángmǎ fēng*	珠穆朗玛峰
mountain	*shān*	山
mountaineering	*dēngshān*	登山
mounting	*zhuāngbiǎo*	装裱
mouth	*zuǐ*	嘴
mouth organ, Chinese	*shēng*	笙
mouthwash	*shùkǒu jì*	漱口剂
move aside (objects)	*bānkāi*	搬开
move aside (people)	*ràngkāi*	让开
movement (music)	*yuèzhāng*	乐章
movie	*diànyǐng*	电影
movie camera	*diànyǐng shèxiàngjī*	电影摄像机
movie star	*yǐngxīng*	影星
Mr.	*xiānsheng*	先生
Mrs.	*tàitai, fūrén*	太太,夫人
Ms.	*nǚshì*	女士
MSG	*wèijīng*	味精
much	*duō*	多
mug	*bēizi*	杯子
mulberry tree	*sāngshù*	桑树
multiply	*chéng*	乘
mung bean	*lǜdòu*	绿豆
mural	*bìhuà*	壁画
muscle	*jīròu*	肌肉
museum	*bówùguǎn*	博物馆

mushroom	*mógu*	蘑菇
music	*yīnyuè*	音乐
musical (show)	*gēwǔjù*	歌舞剧
musical instrument	*yuèqì*	乐器
musical staff, 5-line	*wǔxiànpǔ*	五线谱
must	*bìxū*	必须
mustard(condiment)	*jièmo*	芥末
mustard, leaf	*gàicài*	芥菜
musty	*fāméi*	发霉
mutton	*yángròu*	羊肉
my	*wǒde*	我的
My God!	*wǒde tiān!*	我的天!
nail(hardware)	*dīngzi*	钉子
name (n)	*míngzi*	名字
napkin, paper	*cānjīnzhǐ*	餐巾纸
narcissus	*shuǐxiān*	水仙
narrow	*xiázhǎi*	狭窄
nasal congestion	*bízi bù tōng*	鼻子不通
national(adj)	*guójiā*	国家
notional anthem	*guógē*	国歌
national defense	*guófáng*	国防
national emblem	*guóhuī*	国徽
national flag	*guóqí*	国旗
national guide	*quánpéi*	全陪
nationality(ethnic)	*mínzú*	民族
native place (ancestral)	*lǎojiā*	老家
natural	*zìrán*	自然
nature(character)	*xìnggé*	性格
nature (outdoors)	*dà zìrán*	大自然
nauseous	*ěxīn*	恶心
navy	*hǎihūn*	海军
near	*jìn*	近
nearest	*zuìjìn*	最近
neck	*bózi*	脖子
necklace	*xiàngliàn*	项链
need	*xūyào , yào*	需要,要
needle	*zhēn*	针
needle and thread	*zhēnxiàn*	针线
needlework	*zhēnxiàn huó*	针线活

DICTIONARY

negative(film)	*dǐpiàn*	底片
neighbor	*línjū*	邻居
Neolithic era	*xīn shíqì shídài*	新石器时代
Nepal	*Ní bó'ěr*	泥泊尔
nerve	*shénjīng*	神经
nervous(mood)	*jǐnzhāng*	紧张
Nescafe	*Què cáo*	雀巢
neurology	*shénjīngbìngxué*	神经病学
neurosis	*shénjīngzhì*	神经质
never	*yǒngbù*	永不
never again	*zài yě bù*	再也不
never have	*cóng méi*	从没
new	*xīn*	新
New Wave	*xīncháo*	新潮
New Year	*xīnnián, yuándàn*	新年,元旦
New Year painting	*niánhuà*	年画
New York	*Niǔyuē*	纽约
New Zealand	*Xīnxīlán*	新西兰
New Zealand dollar	*Xīnxīlán yuán*	新西兰元
news	*xīnwén, xiāoxi*	新闻,消息
news program	*xīnwén jiémù*	新闻节目
newspaper	*bàozhǐ*	报纸
newsstand	*bàotíng, bàotān*	报亭,报摊
next (forthcoming)	*xiàyígè, xiàmiànde*	下一个,下面的
next stop	*xiàzhàn*	下站
next time	*xià cì*	下次
next to (at the side of)	*zài...pángbiān*	在……旁边
next year	*míngnián*	明年
nice	*hǎo, bú cuò*	好,不错
night	*yèwǎn*	夜晚
night bus	*yèbānchē*	夜班车
night market	*yèshì*	夜市
night shift	*yèbān*	夜班
nightlife	*yè shēnghuó*	夜生活
nightstand	*chuángtóuguì*	床头柜
Nikon	*Níkāng*	尼康
nine	*jiǔ*	九
ninety	*jiǔshí*	九十
Nissan	*Nísāng*	尼桑
noisy	*chǎo*	吵
nonstaple food	*fùshípǐn*	副食品
noodles	*miàntiáo*	面条

noon	*zhōngwǔ*	中午
north	*běi*	北
North America	*Běiměizhōu*	北美洲
North Pole	*Běijí*	北极
North Star	*Běijí xīng*	北极星
nose	*bízi*	鼻子
not	*bù , méi*	不,没
not bad	*bú cuò*	不错
novel(n)	*xiǎoshuō*	小说
November	*shíyīyuè*	十一月
now	*xiànzài*	现在
nuclear	*hé*	核
numb	*má*	麻
number (numeral)	*hàomǎ*	号码
number (quantity)	*shùzi*	数字
nurse(n)	*hùshì*	护士
nursery school	*tuō' érsuǒ*	托儿所
o'clock	*diǎnzhōng*	点钟
oatmeal	*màipiàn*	麦片
object(thing)	*dōngxi*	东西
observation ward	*guānchá shì*	观察室
ocean	*hǎiyáng*	海洋
October	*shíyuè*	十月
of course	*dāngrán*	当然
office	*bàngōngshì*	办公室
often	*jīngcháng*	经常
Oh well(forget it)	*suànle*	算了
oil	*yóu*	油
oil(petroleum)	*shíyóu*	石油
oil painting	*yóu huà*	油画
ointment	*ruǎngāo*	软膏
okay	*xíng*	行
old(aged)	*lǎo*	老
old(used)	*jiù*	旧
old age	*lǎonián*	老年
old man	*lǎo dàye*	老大爷
old town(section of a city)	*lǎochéng , jiùchéng*	老城,旧城
oleander	*jiāzhútáo*	夹竹桃
olive	*gǎnlǎn*	橄榄
Olympic Games	*Àoyùnhuì*	奥运会

omelet	*dànjiǎo*	蛋饺
one	*yī*	一
one-child policy	*dúshēng zǐnǚ zhèngcè*	独生子女政策
one-way street	*dānxíng xiàn*	单行线
one-way ticket	*dānchéng piào*	单程票
onion	*cōngtóu*	葱头
only	*zhǐ*	只
oolong tea	*wūlóng chá*	乌龙茶
open	*kāi*	开
open-dated ticket	*bú dìngqī piào*	不定期票
open for business	*kāimén*	开门
opera	*gējù*	歌剧
opera mask	*xìjù liǎnpǔ*	戏剧脸谱
opera singer (Chinese opera)	*xìjù yǎnyuán*	戏剧演员
opera singer (Western opera)	*gējù yǎnyuán*	歌剧演员
operation room	*shǒu shùshì*	手术室
operator(phone)	*zǒngjī*	总机
ophthamologist	*yǎnkē yīshēng*	眼科医生
ophthamology department	*yǎn kē*	眼科
opinion	*yìjiàn*	意见
opium	*yāpiàn*	鸦片
opportunity	*jīhuì*	机会
or	*huòzhě, hàishì*	或者,还是
orange(color)	*júhuáng*	桔黄
orange(fruit)	*gānjú, guǎnggān*	柑桔,广柑
orange juice	*júzi zhī*	桔子汁
orange soda	*júzi shuǐ*	桔子水
orchestra	*jiāoxiǎng yuè duì*	交响乐队
orchestra, traditional Chinese	*mínzú yuè duì*	民族乐队
orchid	*lánhuā*	兰花
order(command)	*mìnglìng*	命令
order(for purchase)	*dìnggòu*	订购
order (sequence)	*cìxù*	次序
order food	*diǎncài*	点菜
original(n)	*yuánzuò, yuánjiàn*	原作,原件
ornament	*zhuāngshì*	装饰
other	*biéde*	别的
otter	*shuǐtǎ*	水獭

ounce	àngsī	盎司
our	wǒmende	我们的
outlet(electrical)	chāzuò	插座
outside	wài	外
outstanding	chūsè	出色
overcoat	dàyī	大衣
overpass	tiānqiáo	天桥
overseas Chinese	Huáqiáo	华侨
overseas edition	hǎiwàibǎn	海外版
overture(music)	xùqǔ	序曲
overworked(tired)	láolèi	劳累
owe	qiàn	欠
own	yǒu	有
ox	niú	牛
oxygen	yǎngqì	氧气
oyster	háo	蚝
oyster sauce	háoyóu	蚝油
Pacific Ocean	Tàipíngyáng	太平洋
pack(v)	zhuāng	装
pack suitcases	dǎ xíngli	打行李
package(n)	bāoguǒ	包裹
packaging tape	mìfēngjiāodài	密封胶带
pagoda	tǎ	塔
paid	yǐfù	已付
pain(physical)	téng	疼
pain-killer	zhǐténgyào	止疼药
paint(a picture)	huàhuà	画画
painter(artist)	huàjiā	画家
painting(art)	huìhuà	绘画
painting, traditional Chinese	guóhuà	国画
pajama	shuìyī	睡衣
palace	gōngdiàn	宫殿
palpitation	xīntiào	心跳
pancake(for Peking Duck)	báobǐng	薄饼
panda	xióngmāo	熊猫
pantomime	yǎjù	哑剧
pants	kùzi	裤子
paper	zhǐ	纸
paper clip	zhǐjiā	纸夹

DICTIONARY

papercut(folk art)	jiǎnzhǐ	剪纸
parade(military)	yuèbīng	阅兵
parasol tree, Chinese	wútóngshù	梧桐树
parcel	bāoguǒ	包裹
pardon(an offense)	ráoshù	饶恕
parents	fùmǔ	父母
Paris	Bālí	巴黎
park(a vehicle)	tíng	停
park, public	gōngyuán	公园
parking lot(bikes)	cúnchēchù	存车处
part(not whole)	bùfen	部分
partner	huǒbàn	伙伴
party(gathering)	jùhuì	聚会
party(political)	dǎng	党
party member	dǎngyuán	党员
pass(go beyond)	guò	过
passion	gǎnqíng	感情
passport	hùzhào	护照
past, in the	guòqù	过去
patience	nàixīn	耐心
patient(sick person)	bìngrén	病人
pattern(decorative)	tú'àn	图案
pattern(standard)	guīgé	规格
pavilion	tíngzi	亭子
pay(v)	fùqián	付钱
pea	wāndòu	豌豆
pea-flour cake	wāndòuhuáng	豌豆黄
peace	hépíng	和平
peach	táozi	桃子
peanut	huāshēng	花生
pear	lí	梨
pearl	zhēnzhū	珍珠
pearl cream	zhēnzhūshuāng	珍珠霜
Pearl River	Zhūjiāng	珠江
peasant	nóngmín	农民
pedal(n)	jiǎotàbǎn	脚踏板
peddler	xiǎofàn	小贩
pedestrian	xíngrén	行人
pediatrician	érkēyīshēng	儿科医生
pediatrics department	érkē	儿科
peel(n)	pí	皮

peel(v)	*xiāopí*	削皮
Peking duck	*Běijīngkǎoyā*	北京烤鸭
pen(ball-point)	*yuánzhūbǐ*	圆珠笔
pen(fountain)	*gāngbǐ*	钢笔
pencil	*qiānbǐ*	铅笔
penicillin	*qīngméisù*	青霉素
peony	*mǔdān*	牡丹
people(of a nation)	*rénmín*	人民
People's Daily	*Rénmín Rìbào*	人民日报
pepper(ground)	*hújiāofěn*	胡椒粉
pepper, green	*qīngjiāo*	青椒
pepper, hot	*làjiāo*	辣椒
percent	*bǎifēnzhī...*	百分之……
percussion instrument	*dǎjīyuèqì*	打击乐器
performer	*biǎoyǎnzhě*	表演者
perhaps	*yěxǔ*	也许
permanent wave	*tàngfà*	烫发
permission	*xǔkě , yǔnxǔ*	许可,允许
persimmon	*shìzi*	柿子
person	*rén*	人
person-to-person (phone)	*jiàorén*	叫人
personal effects	*sīréncáichǎn*	私人财产
personality	*xìnggé*	性格
petroleum	*shíyóu*	石油
Peugeot	*Báirú*	白茹
pharmacist	*yàojìshī*	药剂师
pharmacy	*yàofáng*	药房
Philadelphia	*Fèichéng*	费城
Philippines	*Fēilǜbīn*	菲律宾
phoenix	*fènghuáng*	凤凰
phone(see telephone)	*diànhuà*	电话
photo album	*yǐngjí , xiàngcè*	影集,像册
photograph(n)	*zhàopiàn*	照片
photograph(v)	*zhàoxiàng*	照相
photographer	*shèyǐngshī*	摄影师
photography	*shèyǐng*	摄影
physics	*wùlǐ*	物理
piano	*gāngqín*	钢琴
pick(select)	*tiāo*	挑
pick up(get)	*qǔ*	取

DICTIONARY

pick up (meet)	jiē	接
pick up (retrieve from ground)	jiǎn	捡
pickled cabbage, hot	làbáicài	辣白菜
pickled cucumber	suānhuángguā	酸黄瓜
pickled mustard tuber, hot	zhàcài	榨菜
pickled vegetables	pàocài	泡菜
pictorial (magazine)	huàbào	画报
picture	túhuà	图画
picture book	huàcè	画册
piece (n)	kuài, jiàn, gè	块,件,个
pig	zhū	猪
pigeon	gēzi	鸽子
pill	yàowán	药丸
pillar	zhùzi	柱子
pillow	zhěntou	枕头
pillowcase	zhěntoutào	枕头套
pilose antler	lùróng	鹿茸
pilot (airplane)	fēixíngyuán	飞行员
pin (straight pin)	dàtóuzhēn	大头针
pine (tree)	sóngshù	松树
pineapple	bōluó	菠萝
ping-pong	pīngpāngqiú	乒乓球
Pingju Opera	píngjù	评剧
pink	fěnsè	粉色
pint	pìntuō	品脱
place (n)	dìfang	地方
place of interest	kěkàndedìfang	可看的地方
plains	píngyuán	平原
plan	jìhuà, dǎsuàn	计划,打算
plane	fēijī	飞机
plant (botanical)	zhíwù	植物
plaster (medicated)	gāoyào	膏药
plate (dish)	pánzi	盘子
plateau	gāoyuán	高原
platform	píngtái	平台
platform (train station)	yuètái	月台
play (a game)	wán	玩
play (sports: hit)	dǎ	打
play (sports: kick)	tī	踢

play(theater)	*huàjù*	话剧
player(in a game)	*xuǎnshǒu*	选手
player(sports team)	*duìyuán*	队员
playground	*cāochǎng*	操场
playwright	*jùzuòjiā*	剧作家
Please...	*qǐng...*	请……
pleased	*hěngāoxìng*	很高兴
pliers	*qiánzi*	钳子
plot(story)	*qíngjié*	情节
plug(n)	*chātóu*	插头
plum	*lǐzi*	李子
plum blossom	*méihuā*	梅花
pneumonia	*féiyán*	肺炎
poached egg	*wòjīdàn, shuǐpūdàn*	卧鸡蛋,水浦蛋
pocket	*dōu, kǒudài*	兜,口袋
pocket-size	*xiùzhēn*	袖珍
poet	*shīrén*	诗人
poetry	*shī*	诗
poker(game)	*púkè*	扑克
Polaroid camera	*yícìchéngxiàngjī*	一次成相机
Polaroid film	*Pāilìdéxiàngzhǐ*	拍立得相纸
police	*jǐngchá*	警察
police station	*pàichūsuǒ*	派出所
policy	*zhèngcè*	政策
polite	*yǒulǐmào*	有礼貌
political bureau	*zhèngzhìjú*	政治局
politics	*zhèngzhì*	政治
polo	*mǎqiú*	马球
polyester(fiber)	*qínglún*	晴纶
pomegranate	*shíliu*	石榴
pomelo(grapefruit)	*yòuzi*	柚子
poor(not good)	*bùhǎo*	不好
poor(not rich)	*qióng*	穷
popular music	*liúxíngqǔ*	流行曲
porcelain	*cíqì*	瓷器
pork	*zhūròu*	猪肉
pork chop	*zhūpái*	猪排
porridge	*zhōu*	粥
port city	*gǎngwānchéngshì*	港湾城市
portable	*biànxiéshì*	便携式
porter	*xínglǐyuán*	行李员
portrait	*xiāoxiàng*	肖像

DICTIONARY

portray	sùzào	塑造
possibility	kěnéng xíng	可能性
possible	kěnéng	可能
post(to mail)	jì	寄
post office	yóujú	邮局
postcard	míngxìnpiàn	明信片
poster	zhāotiēhuà	招贴画
pot(pan)	guō	锅
Potala Palace	Bùdálā gōng	布达拉宫
potato	tǔdòu	土豆
pottery	táoqì	陶器
pound(weight)	bàng	磅
pound sterling	yīngbàng	英磅
powder	fěnmò	粉末
power(authority)	quánlì	权力
power(energy)	néngyuán	能源
power(force)	lìliàng	力量
practical(realistic)	shíjì	实际
practical(useful)	shíyòng	实用
practice(v)	liànxí	练习
prawn	dà xiā	大虾
pray	qídǎo	祈祷
prefer	gèng xǐhuan	更喜欢
pregnant	huáiyùn	怀孕
premier	zǒnglǐ	总理
prepare	zhǔnbèi	准备
prescription	yàofāng	药方
present(current)	mùqián	目前
president(corporate)	zǒngcái	总裁
president(national)	zǒngtǒng	总统
press(clothing)	tàng	烫
press(push down)	àn	按
pretty	piàoliang	漂亮
pride	zìháo , jiāo'ào	自豪,骄傲
principal(school)	xiàozhǎng	校长
print(art)	bǎnhuà	版画
print(photo)	xiàngpiàn	相片
print(v)	yìn	印
printed matter	yìnshuā pǐn	印刷品
private	sīrén	私人
probably	dàgài	大概
problem	wèntí	问题

process(n)	*guòchéng*	过程
producer	*shēngchǎnzhě*	生产者
product	*chǎnpǐn*	产品
production	*shēngchǎn*	生产
profession	*zhíyè , hángyè*	职业,行业
professor	*jiàoshòu*	教授
program(event)	*jiémù*	节目
program(theater handout)	*jiémù dān*	节目单
prohibited	*jīnzhǐ*	禁止
promise(n)	*nuòyán*	诺言
promise(v)	*dāying*	答应
prop(stage accessory)	*dàojù*	道具
province	*shěng*	省
provincial museum	*shěng bówùguǎn*	省博物馆
prune	*lǐzi fǔ*	李子脯
psychiatrist	*jīngshénbìng yīshēng*	精神病医生
psychologist	*xīnlǐxuéjiā*	心理学家
psychology	*xīnlǐxué*	心理学
psychosis	*jīngshénbìng*	精神病
pub	*jiǔguǎn*	酒馆
public	*gōnggòng*	公共
Public Security Bureau	*gōng'ānjú*	公安局
public bus	*gōnggòng qìchē*	公共汽车
public relations	*gōnggòng guānxì*	公共关系
public square	*guǎngchǎng*	广场
Puer tea	*Pǔ'ěr chá*	普洱茶
pull	*lā*	拉
pullover	*tàotóu shān*	套头衫
pulse	*màibó*	脉搏
punk	*péngké*	朋客
puppet show	*mù'ǒu xì*	木偶戏
pure	*chún*	纯
purple	*zǐsè*	紫色
purpose	*mùdì*	目的
purse	*qiánbāo*	钱包
push	*tuī*	推
put	*fàng*	放
put away(in place)	*fànghǎo*	放好

DICTIONARY

Qin Emperor	*Qínshǐhuáng*	秦始皇
quail	*ānchún*	鹌鹑
quality	*zhìliàng*	质量
quantity	*shùliàng*	数量
quarantine	*jiǎnyì*	检疫
quart	*kuātuō*	夸脱
quarter(one-fourth)	*sìfēn zhīyī*	四分之一
quarter hour	*kè , kèzhōng*	刻,刻钟
quartet	*sìchóngzòu*	四重奏
question(n)	*wèntí*	问题
question(v)	*tíwèn*	提问
quick	*kuài*	快
quiet	*ānjìng*	安静
quilt	*bèizi*	被子
quinine	*kuíníng*	奎宁
quite	*xiāngdāng*	相当
quota	*dìng'é*	定额
rabbit	*tùzi*	兔子
racket(paddle)	*qiúpāi*	球拍
radiator	*nuǎnqì*	暖气
radio(broadcast)	*guǎngbō*	广播
radio(machine)	*shōuyīnjī*	收音机
radio program	*guǎngbō jiémù*	广播节目
radiologist	*fàngshèkē yīshī*	放射科医师
radish	*xiǎo luóbo*	小罗卜
railroad	*tiělù*	铁路
railway station	*huǒchēzhàn*	火车站
rain(n)	*yǔ*	雨
rain(v)	*xiàyǔ*	下雨
rain poncho	*yǔpī*	雨披
rainbow	*cǎihóng*	彩虹
raincoat	*yǔyī*	雨衣
raise(lift up)	*tái qǐlai*	抬起来
raisin	*pútáo gān*	葡萄干
ram	*yáng , shānyáng*	羊,山羊
ramie	*zhùmá*	苎麻
rape(vegetable)	*yóucài*	油菜
rash(on skin)	*pízhěn*	皮疹
rat	*lǎoshǔ*	老鼠
rate(price)	*jiàgé*	价格
rather(prefer to)	*nìngyuàn*	宁愿

ratio	*bǐlì*	比例
ravioli(boiled dumplings)	*jiǎozi*	饺子
rayon	*rénzào sī*	人造丝
razor	*tìdāo*	剃刀
razor blade	*dāopiàn*	刀片
read	*dú, kàn*	读,看
read aloud	*niàn*	念
read books	*kàn shū*	看书
real	*zhēn*	真
real estate agent	*dìchǎn jīngjìrén*	地产经纪人
really	*zhēnde*	真的
reason(cause)	*yuányīn*	原因
reason(logic)	*dàoli*	道理
receipt(sales slip)	*fāpiào*	发票
receive(goods)	*shōu*	收
recently	*jìnlái*	近来
reception	*jiēdài*	接待
reception desk	*jiē dài chù*	接待处
reception personnel	*jiēdài rényuán*	接待人员
reception room	*jiēdài shì*	接待室
recipe(cooking)	*shípǔ*	食谱
recipient	*shōujiàn rén, duìfāng*	收件人,对方
recite	*bèi*	背
recommend	*tuījiàn*	推荐
record store	*yīnxiǎng ménshìbù*	音响门市部
recreation room	*yùlè shì*	娱乐室
red	*hóng*	红
red-crowned crane	*dāndǐnghè*	丹顶鹤
red paste(for seals)	*yìnní*	印泥
red wine	*hóngjiǔ*	红酒
reference(for study)	*cānkǎo*	参考
reform	*gǎigé*	改革
refreshment (cold drinks)	*lěngyǐn*	冷饮
refreshment(snacks)	*xiǎochī*	小吃
refreshment stand	*xiǎochī tān*	小吃摊
refrigerator	*bīngxiāng*	冰箱
refund	*péicháng, péi*	赔偿,赔
region	*dìqū*	地区
register	*dēngjì*	登记

DICTIONARY

registered(mail)	guàhào	挂号
registration desk	dēngjì chù	登记处
registration office (hospital)	guàhào chù	挂号处
regret	hòuhuǐ	后悔
regulation	guīdìng	规定
rehearsal	páiliàn	排练
relative(kin)	qīnqī	亲戚
relatives(kinfolk)	qīnshǔ	亲属
relevance	guānxi	关系
relief(sculpture)	fúdiāo	浮雕
remain(stay)	liú	留
remember	jìde	记得
Renault	Léinuò	雷诺
rent(v)	zū	租
rental fee	zūjīn	租金
repair	xiū lǐ	修理
repeat	chóngfù	重复
reprint(v)	jiāyìn	加印
reproduction (replica)	fùzhìpǐn	复制品
request	yāoqiú	要求
reroute	gǎihuàn	改换
research institute	yánjiūsuǒ	研究所
resemble	xiàng	像
reservations desk	yùdìng chù	预订处
reserve(v)	yùdìng	预订
reside	zhù	住
residence permit	jūliú zhèng	居留证
respect	zūnjìng	尊敬
rest(relax)	xiūxi	休息
restaurant	fànguǎn , cāntīng	饭馆,餐厅
result	jiéguǒ	结果
retail	língshòu	零售
retired worker	tuìxiū gōngrén	退休工人
return(come back)	huí	回
return(give back)	huán	还
return(merchandise)	tuì	退
reunion	tuánjù	团聚
review(critique)	pínglùn	评论
review(study again)	fùxí	复习
revolution	gémìng	革命

rheumatism	*fēngshī bìng*	风湿病
rib (n)	*lèigǔ*	肋骨
rice (cooked)	*mǐfàn*	米饭
rice (crop)	*dàozi*	稻子
rice congee	*xīfàn*	稀饭
rice paper	*xuānzhǐ*	宣纸
rich (prosperous)	*fù*	富
ride (a bicycle)	*qí*	骑
ride (a car)	*zuò*	坐
ride (an animal)	*qí*	骑
right (correct)	*duì*	对
right (direction)	*yòu*	右
right away	*mǎshàng*	马上
ring (jewelry)	*jièzhi*	戒指
riot	*bàoluàn*	暴乱
rise (go up, increase)	*shàngshēng*	上升
river	*hé , jiāng*	河,江
road	*lù , mǎlù*	路,马路
roadside	*lùbiān*	路边
roast (v)	*kǎo*	烤
roast pork bun	*chāshāo bāo*	叉烧包
roast suckling pig	*rǔzhū*	乳猪
rock-and-roll	*yáogǔn yuè*	摇滚乐
roll (n)	*juǎn*	卷
Rome	*Luómǎ*	罗马
roof	*fángdǐng*	房顶
room (in a building)	*fángjiān*	房间
room number	*fánghào*	房号
roommate	*tóngwū*	同屋
rooster	*gōngjī*	公鸡
rope skipping (Chinese)	*tiào píjīn*	跳皮筋
rose (flower)	*méiguìhuā*	玫瑰花
rose, Chinese	*yuèjì*	月季
rough	*cūcāo*	粗糙
round (shape)	*yuán*	圆
round-trip ticket	*láihuí piào*	来回票
route	*lù*	路
row (column, line)	*pái*	排
rowboat	*xiǎochuán*	小船
rowing (sport)	*huátǐng*	划艇
rubbing alcohol	*yīyòng jiǔjīng*	医用酒精

rude	*cūbào*	粗暴
rug	*dìtǎn*	地毯
ruins	*yízhǐ*	遗址
ruler (measuring) (stick)	*chǐzi*	尺子
runny nose	*liú bítì*	流鼻涕
rural	*nóngcūn*	农村
rush service	*jiājí fúwù*	加急服务
Russian (language)	*Éyǔ*	俄语
rusty	*xiù le*	锈了
sable	*zǐdiāo*	紫貂
Sacred Way	*shéndào*	神道
safety pin	*biézhēn*	别针
salad	*shālā*	沙拉
salary	*gōngzī*	工资
sales counter	*shòuhuò tái, guìtái*	售货台,柜台
sales manager	*xiāoshòu jīnglǐ*	销售经理
salesperson	*tuīxiāoyuán*	推销员
saline solution	*shēnglǐ yánshuǐ*	生理盐水
saliva	*kǒushuǐ*	口水
salt	*yán*	盐
salted duck egg	*xián yādàn*	咸鸭蛋
salty	*xián*	咸
same	*yíyàng*	一样
sample good	*yàngpǐn*	样品
San Francisco	*Jiùjīnshān*	旧金山
sand	*shāzi*	沙子
sandals	*liángxié*	凉鞋
sandalwood fan	*tánxiāng shàn*	檀香扇
sandwich	*sānmíngzhì*	三明治
sanitary napkin	*wèishēng jīn*	卫生巾
Santana	*Sāngtǎnà*	桑塔纳
satellite	*wèixīng*	卫星
satisfied	*mǎnyì*	满意
satisfy	*mǎnzú*	满足
Saturday	*xīngqī liù*	星期六
sauce	*jiàng*	酱
sausage	*xiāngcháng*	香肠
sauteed	*chǎo*	炒
say	*shuō*	说
scallion	*cōng*	葱

scallop	*gānbèi*	干贝
scarf	*wéijīn*	围巾
scarlet fever	*xīnghóngrè*	猩红热
scenery	*fēngjǐng*	风景
schedule (timetable)	*shíkè biǎo*	时刻表
schizophrenia	*jīngshén fēnliè zhèng*	精神分裂症
school	*xuéxiào*	学校
school (of thought)	*liúpài*	流派
science	*kēxué*	科学
scientist	*kēxuéjiā*	科学家
scissors	*jiǎndāo*	剪刀
scrambled eggs	*chǎo jīdàn*	炒鸡蛋
screen (n)	*píngfēng*	屏风
screw (n)	*luósīdīng*	螺丝钉
screwdriver	*luósīdāo*	螺丝刀
script (play or film)	*jiǎoběn*	脚本
sculptor	*diāosù jiā*	雕塑家
sculpture	*diāosù*	雕塑
sea	*hǎi*	海
sea cucumber	*hǎishēn*	海参
seafood	*hǎixiān*	海鲜
season (n)	*jìjié*	季节
seat (n)	*zuòwèi*	座位
seat number	*zuòhào*	座号
seatbelt	*ānquándài*	安全带
second (fraction of time)	*miǎo*	秒
secret	*mìmì*	秘密
secretariat	*shūjìchù*	书记处
secretary, office	*mìshū*	秘书
security guard	*ānquán rényuán*	安全人员
see	*kànjiàn*	看见
see off	*sòng*	送
See you later	*huítóujiàn*	回头见
seems	*hǎoxiàng*	好像
self	*zìjǐ, zìgě*	自己,自个儿
self-portrait	*zìhuàxiàng*	自画像
self-timer (camera)	*zìpāi*	自拍
sell	*mài*	卖
seminar	*yántǎohuì*	研讨会
send a telegram	*fā diànbào*	发电报
send a telex	*fā diànchuán*	发电传

DICTIONARY

senior citizen	*lǎoniánrén*	老年人
sentence (n)	*jùzi*	句子
Seoul	*Hànchéng*	汉城
September	*jiǔyuè*	九月
serious (earnest)	*rènzhēn*	认真
serious (grave)	*yánzhòng*	严重
servant	*púrén*	仆人
service	*fúwù*	服务
service attendant	*fúwùyuán*	服务员
service desk	*fúwùtái*	服务台
service fee	*fúwùfèi*	服务费
service, religious	*lǐbài*	礼拜
sesame biscuit	*shāobǐng*	烧饼
sesame oil	*máyóu*	麻油
set (matching pieces)	*tào*	套
set (theater)	*bùjǐng*	布景
set design	*bùjǐng shèjì*	布景设计
settle the bill	*jiézhàng*	结帐
seven	*qī*	七
seventy	*qīshí*	七十
several	*hǎo jǐgè*	好几个
sew	*féng*	缝
sex	*xìng*	性
shadow	*yǐng*	影
shadow puppet	*píyǐng*	皮影
shake hands	*wòshǒu*	握手
shampoo	*xiāngbō*	香波
Shanghai Opera	*hùjù*	沪剧
Shangri-La	*Xiānggélǐlā*	香格里拉
Shaoxing Opera	*yuèjù, Shàoxīng xì*	越剧, 绍兴戏
Shaoxing rice wine	*Shàoxīng jiāfàn jiǔ*	绍兴加饭酒
share (an expense)	*fēntān*	分摊
shark's fin soup	*yúchì tāng*	鱼翅汤
sharp (edge)	*fēnglì*	锋利
shattered	*suì le*	碎了
shave	*guāliǎn*	刮脸
shaver, electric	*diàn tìdāo*	电剃刀
she	*tā*	她
sheep	*yáng*	羊
sheet (of paper)	*zhāng*	张
sheets (linen)	*chuángdān*	床单
shelf	*jiàzi*	架子

shell mosaic	*bèidiāohuà*	贝雕画
Sheraton	*Xǐláidēng*	喜来登
shiny	*shǎnguāng*	闪光
ship (n)	*chuán*	船
ship (v)	*hǎiyùn*	海运
shipping company	*hángyùn gōngsī*	航运公司
shirt	*chènshān*	衬衫
shiver	*fādǒu*	发抖
shock (n)	*xiūkè*	休克
shoe	*xié*	鞋
shoe polish	*xiéyóu*	鞋油
shoehorn	*xiébázi*	鞋拔子
shoelaces	*xiédài*	鞋带
shooting (sport)	*shèjī*	射击
shop (n)	*shāngdiàn，pùzi*	商店,铺子
shopping	*mǎi dōngxi*	买东西
short (height)	*ǎi*	矮
short (length)	*duǎn*	短
should	*yīnggāi*	应该
shoulder (n)	*jiānbǎng*	肩膀
shoulder bag	*bēibāo*	背包
show (performance)	*biǎoyǎn，yǎnchū*	表演,演出
show (to demonstrate)	*shìfàn*	示范
shower	*línyù*	淋浴
shower cap	*línyù mào*	淋浴帽
shredded dried meat	*ròusōng*	肉松
shrimp	*xiā*	虾
shrine	*jìtán*	祭坛
shut	*guān，bì*	关,闭
shutter (camera)	*kuàimén*	快门
Siberia	*Xībólìyà*	西伯利亚
sickness	*bìng*	病
side (body)	*cèlèi*	侧肋
side (margin)	*biān*	边
sidewalk	*rénxíngdào*	人行道
sightsee	*guānguāng，yóulǎn*	观光,游览
sign (notice board)	*páizi*	牌子
sign (symbol)	*biāojì*	标记
signature	*qiānmíng*	签名
silent	*wúshēng*	无声
silk (pure)	*zhēnsī*	真丝

DICTIONARY

silk and brocade factory	*sīzhī chàng*	丝织厂
silk cocoon factory	*sāosī chǎng*	缫丝厂
silk fabric	*sīchóu*	丝绸
silk mill	*sīchóu chǎng*	丝绸厂
silk products shop	*sīchóu shāngdiàn*	丝绸商店
Silk Road	*Sīchóu zhīlù*	丝绸之路
silkworm	*cán*	蚕
silver	*yín*	银
simulate	*mónǐ*	模拟
sing	*chànggē*	唱歌
Singapore	*Xīnjiāpō*	新加坡
singer	*gēchàng jiā*	歌唱家
single room	*dānjiān*	单间
sink	*shuǐchízi*	水池子
sister (older)	*jiějie*	姐姐
sister (younger)	*mèimei*	妹妹
sit	*zuò*	坐
six	*liù*	六
sixty	*liùshí*	六十
size (measurement)	*chǐcùn, guīgé*	尺寸, 规格
size (number)	*hào*	号
sketch (art)	*sùxiě*	速写
sketch (design draft)	*cǎotú*	草图
skiing	*huáxuě*	滑雪
skill	*jìqiǎo*	技巧
skin	*pífū*	皮肤
skirt	*qúnzi*	裙子
sky	*tiānkōng*	天空
sky-diving	*tiàosǎn*	跳伞
sleep (v)	*shuìjiào*	睡觉
sleeping pill	*ānmián yào*	安眠药
slice (n)	*piàn*	片
slide (photo)	*huàndēng piàn*	幻灯片
slide film	*fǎnzhuǎn piàn*	反转片
slide mount	*huàndēngpiàn kuàng*	幻灯片框
slip (petticoat)	*chènqún*	衬裙
slippers	*tuōxié*	拖鞋
slow	*màn*	慢
small	*xiǎo*	小
smell (n)	*wèidao, wèi*	味道, 味
smell (v)	*wén*	闻

smile	*wēixiào*	微笑
smoke cigarettes	*chōuyān*	抽烟
smoked fish	*xūnyú*	熏鱼
snack	*xiǎochī, diǎnxin*	小吃,点心
snake	*shé*	蛇
snow (n)	*xuě*	雪
snow (v)	*xiàxuě*	下雪
snow mountain	*xuěshān*	雪山
snow peas	*xuědòu*	雪豆
snuff bottle	*bíyānhú*	鼻烟壶
snuff box	*bíyānhé*	鼻烟盒
so (therefore)	*suǒyǐ*	所以
so-so	*yìbān, mǎmǎhūhū*	一般,马马虎虎
soap (n)	*féizào*	肥皂
soccer	*zúqiú*	足球
soccer match	*zúqiú bǐsài*	足球比赛
social dancing	*jiāojì wǔ*	交际舞
sociology	*shèhuìxué*	社会学
socket (electrical)	*chāzuò*	插座
socks	*wàzi*	袜子
soda pop	*qìshuǐ*	汽水
soda water	*sūdá shuǐ*	苏打水
sofa	*shāfā*	沙发
soft-seat	*ruǎnxí*	软席
soft-sleeper	*ruǎnwò*	软卧
softball	*lěiqiú*	垒球
soil (n)	*tǔ, tǔrǎng*	土,土壤
soldier	*shìbīng, jūnrén*	士兵,军人
solo (dance)	*dúwǔ*	独舞
solo (instrumental)	*dúzòu*	独奏
solo (vocal)	*dúchàng*	独唱
solution (method)	*bànfǎ*	办法
solve	*jiějué*	解决
some	*yìxiē*	一些
sometimes	*yǒushí*	有时
son	*érzi*	儿子
sonata	*zòumíngqǔ*	奏鸣曲
song	*gēqǔ*	歌曲
song-and-dance	*gēwǔ*	歌舞
song-and-dance troupe	*gēwǔ tuán*	歌舞团
Sony	*Suǒní*	索尼

DICTIONARY

soon	*mǎshàng, yīhuìr*	马上,一会儿
sore (ache)	*fāsuān, suān*	发酸,酸
sore throat	*hóulóng téng*	喉咙疼
soreness	*suānténg*	酸疼
sorghum	*gāoliáng*	高粱
sound (n)	*shēngyīn*	声音
sound effect	*yīnxiǎng*	音响
soup	*tāng*	汤
soup noodles	*tāngmiàn*	汤面
sour	*suān*	酸
south	*nán*	南
South America	*Nánměizhōu*	南美洲
South China Sea	*Nánhǎi*	南海
Soviet Union	*Sūlián*	(前)苏联
soy sauce	*jiàngyóu*	酱油
soybean	*huángdòu*	黄豆
soybean milk	*dòujiāng*	豆浆
space	*kōngjiān*	空间
space shuttle	*hángtiān fēijī*	航天飞机
spare time	*yèyú shíjiān*	业余时间
sparerib	*páigǔ*	排骨
speak	*jiǎng*	讲
special delivery (mail)	*kuàidì*	快递
speed limit	*xiàn sù*	限速
spend	*huā*	花
spicy (hot)	*là*	辣
spinach	*bōcài*	菠菜
spine	*jǐzhuī*	脊椎
splinter (n)	*cì*	刺
spoke (wheel)	*chētiáo*	车条
spoon	*sháozi*	勺子
sporting goods	*tǐyù yòngpǐn*	体育用品
sports	*yùndòng*	运动
sports event	*yùndòng xiàngmù*	运动项目
spotlight	*jùguāngdēng*	聚光灯
spouse	*pèi'ǒu*	配偶
sprained	*niǔshāng*	扭伤
spring (season)	*chūntiān*	春天
spring roll	*chūnjuǎn*	春卷
square (area measure)	*píngfāng*	平方
square (shape)	*fāng*	方
square meter	*píngfāng gōnglǐ*	平方公里

squid	*yóuyú*	鱿鱼
stadium	*tǐyùchǎng*	体育场
stage (n)	*wǔtái*	舞台
stage (of progress)	*jiēduàn*	阶段
stainless steel	*búxiùgāng*	不锈钢
stairs	*lóutī*	楼梯
stale	*bù xīnxiān*	不新鲜
stamp (postage)	*yóupiào*	邮票
stamp collecting	*jíyóu*	集邮
stand (n)	*jiàzi*	架子
stand (v)	*zhàn*	站
standard	*biāozhǔn*	标准
standing committee	*chángwù wěiyuánhuì*	常务委员会
star (celebrity)	*míngxīng*	明星
star (n)	*xīngxing*	星星
state council	*guówùyuàn*	国务院
station (depot)	*zhàn*	站
station-to-station (phone)	*jiàohào*	叫号
stationery (writing paper)	*xìnzhǐ*	信纸
statue	*sùxiàng , diāoxiàng*	塑像,雕像
stay (live, spend time)	*dāi*	呆
steak (beef)	*niúpái*	牛排
steam (v)	*zhēng*	蒸
steamed bun	*mántou*	馒头
steamed dumpling	*bāozi*	包子
steamed twisted roll	*huājuǎn*	花卷
steel	*gāng*	钢
steep (in hot water)	*pào*	泡
steering wheel	*fāngxiàngpán*	方向盘
stele	*shíbǎn , shízuò*	石板,石柱
step (footstep)	*bù*	步
stereo system	*zǔhé yīnxiǎng*	组合音响
stew (v)	*dùn*	炖
stiff	*jiāngyìng*	僵硬
still (further)	*hái*	还
still (motionless)	*bú dòng , tíngzhǐ*	不动,停止
still (yet)	*yīrán , réngrán*	依然,仍然
still life painting	*jìngwù huà*	静物画
stir-fry	*chǎo*	炒
Stockholm	*Sīdégē'ěrmó*	斯德哥尔摩

DICTIONARY

stockings	*chángtǒng wà*	长筒袜
stocks (shares)	*gǔpiào*	股票
stomach	*wèi , dùzi*	胃,肚子
stomachache	*wèiténg*	胃疼
stone (n)	*shítou*	石头
Stone Forest	*Shílín*	石林
stone rubbing	*tàpiàn*	拓片
stop (station)	*zhàn*	站
stop (v)	*tíng*	停
store (put away)	*cúnfàng*	存放
store (shop)	*diàn , shāngdiàn*	店,商店
storyteller	*shuōshū rén*	说书人
storytelling	*shuōshū*	说书
straight	*zhí*	直
straits (waterway)	*hǎixiá*	海峡
strange	*qíguài*	奇怪
stranger (person)	*mòshēng rén*	陌生人
strawberry	*cǎoméi*	草莓
street	*jiē*	街
strength	*lìliang , lìqi*	力量,力气
strict	*yán*	严
string (n)	*shéngzi*	绳子
string bean	*sìjìdòu*	四季豆
string instrument	*xián yuèqì*	弦乐器
string quartet	*xiányuè sìchóngzòu*	弦乐四重奏
striped	*yǒu tiáowén de*	有条纹的
stroke (paralysis)	*zhòngfēng*	中风
strong	*qiángliè*	强烈
struggle	*dòuzhēng*	斗争
stuck	*dǔzhù le*	堵住了
student	*xuéshēng*	学生
study (v)	*xué*	学
study abroad	*liúxué*	留学
stuffy (unventilated)	*mēn*	闷
stupid	*bèn , chǔn*	笨,蠢
sturdy	*jiēshi*	结实
style	*fēnggé*	风格
suburb	*jiāoqū*	郊区
subway	*dìtiě*	地铁
subway station	*dìtiě chēzhàn*	地铁车站
success	*chénggōng*	成功
sugar	*táng*	糖

sugar cane	*gānzhe*	甘蔗
suit (clothing)	*xīzhuāng*	西装
suitcase	*xiāngzi*	箱子
suite (room)	*tàojiān*	套间
sulfa	*huáng'ān*	磺胺
summer	*xiàtiān*	夏天
Summer Palace	*Yíhéyuán*	颐和园
sun	*tàiyang*	太阳
Sun Yat-sen	*Sūn Zhōngshān*	孙中山
Sunday	*xīngqī rì*	星期日
sunlight	*yángguāng*	阳光
sunrise	*rìchū*	日出
sunset	*rìluò*	日落
sunstroke	*zhòngshǔ*	中暑
supervisor	*jiāndū rén*	监督人
support (an endeavor)	*zhīchí*	支持
surface mail	*píngxìn*	平信
surgeon	*wàikē yīshēng*	外科医生
surgery	*shǒushù*	手术
surgery department	*wàikē*	外科
surprised	*jīngyà*	惊讶
sutra	*fójīng*	佛经
swallow (v)	*yàn*	咽
sweat (n)	*hàn*	汗
sweat (v)	*chūhàn*	出汗
sweater	*máoyī*	毛衣
sweatpants	*róngkù*	绒裤
sweatshirt	*róngyī*	绒衣
Sweden	*Ruìdiǎn*	瑞典
sweep	*sǎo*	扫
sweet	*tián*	甜
sweet-and-sour	*tángcù*	糖醋
sweet-and-sour pork	*gǔlǎo ròu*	古老肉
sweet potato	*báishǔ, shānyù*	白薯,山芋
swelling	*zhǒngzhàng*	肿胀
swim	*yóuyǒng*	游泳
swimming pool	*yóuyǒngchí*	游泳池
swimsuit	*yóuyǒngyī*	游泳衣
swing (playground)	*qiūqiān*	秋千
switchboard operator	*zǒngjī*	总机
Switzerland	*Ruìshì*	瑞士
sword bean	*dāodòu*	刀豆

DICTIONARY

English	Pinyin	Chinese
Sydney	*Xīní*	悉尼
symbol	*biāozhì*	标志
symbolize	*xiàngzhēng*	象征
sympathetic	*tóngqíng*	同情
symphony	*jiāoxiǎng yuè*	交响乐
symphony orchestra	*jiāoxiǎng yuèduì*	交响乐队
symptom	*zhèngzhuàng*	症状
synthetic (fiber)	*huàxiān*	化纤
syrup	*tángjiāng*	糖浆
system	*xìtǒng*	系统
T-intersection	*dīngzì lùkǒu*	丁字路口
T-shirt	*duǎnxiù shān*	短袖衫
table (n)	*zhuōzi*	桌子
tablecloth	*táibù, zhuōbù*	台布,桌布
tablespoon	*tóngsháo*	铜勺
tablet	*yàopiàn*	药片
taillight	*wěidēng*	尾灯
tailor (n)	*cáifeng*	裁缝
Taipei	*Táiběi*	台北
Taiwan	*táiwān*	台湾
take (hold)	*ná*	拿
take (medication)	*fúyào*	服药
take a picture	*zhào zhāng xiàng*	照张相
take away	*názǒu*	拿走
take interest in	*duì . . . gǎn xìngqù*	对……感兴趣
take off (flights)	*qǐfēi*	起飞
talk (converse)	*tánhuà, jiāotán*	谈话,交谈
tamer	*xùnshòu yuán*	驯兽员
tampon	*wèishēng shuān*	卫生栓
Tang figurine (tri-colored)	*tángsāncǎi*	唐三彩
tangerine	*júzi*	橘子
tango	*tàngē*	探戈
Taoism	*dàojiào*	道教
tap (faucet)	*shuǐ lóngtóu*	水龙头
tape (cellophane)	*tòumíng jiāodài*	透明胶带
tape (sound)	*lùyīn cídài*	录音磁带
tape measure	*juǎnchǐ*	卷尺
tape recorder	*lùyīnjī*	录音机
tapestry	*bìtǎn*	壁毯
taro	*yùtou*	芋头

taste (n)	*wèidao*	味道
taste (v)	*cháng*	尝
tax (n)	*shuì*	税
taxi (n)	*chūzū qìchē*	出租汽车
tea	*chá*	茶
tea plantation (factory)	*cháchǎng*	茶场
tea set	*chájù*	茶具
tea shop	*cháye diàn*	茶叶店
teach	*jiāo*	教
teacher	*lǎoshī, jiàoshī*	老师,教师
teacup	*chábēi*	茶杯
teapot	*cháhú*	茶壶
teaspoon	*xiǎo tóngsháo*	小铜勺
technician	*jìshùyuán*	技术员
telegram	*diànbào*	电报
telephone (n)	*diànhuà*	电话
telephone (v)	*dǎ diànhuà*	打电话
telephone number	*diànhuà hàomǎ*	电话号码
television	*diànshì*	电视
television set	*diànshìjī*	电视机
television station	*diànshì tái*	电视台
telex	*diànchuán*	电传
telex call number	*diànchuán guàhào*	电传挂号
telex machine	*diànchuánjī*	电传机
tell	*gào sù*	告诉
temperature (general)	*wēndù*	温度
temperature (of body)	*tǐwēn*	体温
temple (Buddhist)	*sì, miào*	寺,庙
temple (Taoist)	*guàn*	观
Temple of Heaven	*Tiāntán*	天坛
ten	*shí*	十
ten thousand	*wàn*	万
tendon	*jīn*	筋
tennis	*wǎngqiú*	网球
terracotta figure	*bīngmǎyǒng*	兵马俑
terrible	*kěpà, zāogāo*	可怕,糟糕
test (exam)	*kǎoshì*	考试
tetanus	*pò shāngfēng*	破伤风
textile	*fǎngzhī pǐn*	纺织品
Thailand	*Tàiguó*	泰国
thank you	*xièxie*	谢谢

DICTIONARY

that	*nà*	那
that one	*nàge, nèige*	那个
theater	*jùchǎng*	剧场
theater troupe	*jùtuán*	剧团
their	*tāmende*	他们的
them	*tāmen*	他们
there	*nàli, nàr*	那里,那儿
therefore	*yīncǐ*	因此
thermal pants	*miánmáo kù*	棉毛裤
thermal shirt	*miánmáo shān*	棉毛衫
thermometer	*wēndù biǎo*	温度表
thermos	*nuǎnshuǐpíng*	暖水瓶
these	*zhèxiē*	这些
they	*tāmen*	他们
thick (coarse)	*cū*	粗
thick (dense)	*nóng*	浓
thick (layer)	*hòu*	厚
thin (layer)	*báo*	薄
thin (slender)	*shòu, xì*	瘦,细
thin (sparse)	*xī*	稀
thing	*dōngxi*	东西
think (believe)	*rènwéi*	认为
thirsty	*kě*	渴
thirty	*sānshí*	三十
this	*zhè*	这
this one	*zhège, zhèige*	这个
this year	*jīnnián*	今年
those	*nàxiē, nèixiē*	那些
thousand	*qiān*	千
thousand-year egg	*pídàn, sōnghuādàn*	皮蛋,松花蛋
thread (n)	*xiàn*	线
three	*sān*	三
three Gorges	*Sānxiá*	三峡
three delicacies soup	*sānxiān tāng*	三鲜汤
three-dimensional	*lìtǐ*	立体
three-prong plug	*sānxiàng chātóu*	三相插头
throat	*hóulóng*	喉咙
throw	*rēng*	扔
throw away	*rēng diào*	扔掉
thunder	*léi*	雷
Thursday	*xīngqī sì*	星期四
Tibet	*Xīzàng*	西藏

ticket	*piào*	票
ticket office	*shòupiào chù*	售票处
ticket seller	*shòupiàoyuán*	售票员
tie (necktie)	*lǐngdài*	领带
tie up	*kǔn qilai*	捆起来
tiger	*lǎohǔ*	老虎
tiger balm	*qīngliángyóu*	清凉油
tight	*jǐn*	紧
tile (n)	*wǎ*	瓦
timber	*mùliào*	木料
time (n)	*shíjiān*	时间
time (occasion)	*cì*	次
time period (historic)	*niándài*	年代
timer	*jìshí qì*	计时器
timetable	*shíkè biǎo*	时刻表
tip (gratuity)	*xiǎofèi*	小费
tire (wheel)	*chētāi*	车胎
tired	*lèi*	累
toast (bread)	*kǎo miànbāo*	烤面包
today	*jīntiān*	今天
toe	*jiǎozhǐ*	脚趾
toilet	*cèsuǒ*	厕所
toilet paper	*wèishēng zhǐ*	卫生纸
Tokyo	*Dōngjīng*	东京
tomato	*xīhóngshì*, *fānqié*	西红柿,番茄
tomato sauce	*fānqié jiàng*	番茄酱
tomb	*fénmù*	坟墓
tombs, imperial	*líng*	陵
tomorrow	*míngtiān*	明天
ton	*dūn*	吨
tongue	*shétou*	舌头
tonight	*jīnwǎn*	今晚
too (also)	*yě*	也
too (excessive)	*tài*	太
tool	*gōngjù*	工具
tooth	*yá*	牙
toothache	*yáténg*	牙疼
toothbrush	*yáshuā*	牙刷
toothpaste	*yágāo*	牙膏
toothpick	*yáqiān*	牙签
top (height)	*dǐng*	顶

DICTIONARY

torn	*pòle*	破了
Toronto	*Duōlúnduō*	多伦多
tortoise	*wūguī*	乌龟
touch-me-not	*fèngxiānhuā*	凤仙花
tour escort	*lǐngduì*	领队
tour group	*lǚyóu tuán*	旅游团
tourist	*lǚkè*	旅客
tournament	*bǐsài*	比赛
toward	*wǎng，xiàng*	往，向
towel	*máojīn*	毛巾
town	*zhèn*	镇
township	*xiāng*	乡
toy	*wánjù*	玩具
toy store	*wánjù diàn*	玩具店
Toyota	*Fēngtián*	丰田
track and field	*tiánjìng*	田径
tractor	*tuōlājī*	拖拉机
trade (business)	*màoyì*	贸易
traditional	*chuántǒng*	传统
traffic	*jiāotōng*	交通
traffic circle	*jiāotōng huándǎo*	交通环岛
traffic jam	*dǔchē*	堵车
traffic light	*hónglǜdēng*	红绿灯
tragedy	*bēijù*	悲剧
train (railroad)	*huǒchē*	火车
train station	*huǒchē zhàn*	火车站
training	*xùnliàn*	训练
tranquilizer	*zhènjìngjì*	镇静剂
transfer (bus, train)	*dǎo，huàn*	倒，换
transformer (voltage)	*biànyāqì*	变压器
transit visa	*guòjìng qiānzhèng*	过境签证
translate	*fānyì*	翻译
translator	*fānyì*	翻译
transparent	*tòumíng*	透明
travel	*lǚxíng*	旅行
travel permit	*lǚyóu xǔkězhèng*	旅游许可证
travel service (agency)	*lǚxíngshè*	旅行社
traveler's check	*lǚxíng zhīpiào*	旅行支票
traveling bag	*lǚxíng bāo*	旅行包
tree	*shù*	树
tribe	*bùluò，jiāzú*	部落，家族

trick (v)	*piàn*	骗
tricycle (child's)	*értóng chē*	儿童车
tricycle (pedicab)	*sānlún chē*	三轮车
trim	*xiūjiǎn*	修剪
trio (instrumental)	*sānchóngzòu*	三重奏
trip (travel)	*lǚxíng*	旅行
tripod	*sānjiǎojià*	三角架
trolley	*wúguǐ diànchē*	无轨电车
truck (n)	*kǎchē*	卡车
true	*zhēn*	真
trunk (car)	*xíngli xiāng*	行李箱
trunk (luggage)	*píxiāng*	皮箱
truth	*zhēnlǐ*	真理
try	*shì yíxià*	试一下
tuberculosis	*fèi jiéhé*	肺结核
Tuesday	*xīngqī èr*	星期二
tug of war	*báhé*	拔河
turn (a corner)	*guǎiwān*	拐湾
turn around (head back)	*diàotóu, huízhuǎn*	调头，回转
turn off (to shut off)	*guān*	关
turn on (to switch on)	*kāi*	开
turnip	*luóbo*	萝卜
turtle	*wūguī*	乌龟
twenty	*èrshí*	二十
twin bed	*dānrén chuáng*	单人床
twin room	*shuāngrén fángjiān*	双人房间
two (the number)	*èr*	二
two (the quantity)	*liǎng*	两
two-prong plug (flat prongs)	*píngjiǎo chātóu*	平角插头
two-prong plug (round prongs)	*yuánjiǎo chātóu*	圆角插头
type (kind)	*zhǒnglèi*	种类
typewriter	*dǎzìjī*	打字机
typhoid	*shānghán*	伤寒
typhoon	*táifēng*	台风
typhus	*bānzhěn shānghán*	斑疹伤寒
typist	*dǎzìyuán*	打字员

DICTIONARY

ugly	*chǒu , nánkàn*	丑,难看
ulcer	*kuìyáng*	溃疡
umbrella	*yǔsǎn*	雨伞
uncle	*shūshu*	叔叔
(see Appendix H)		
under	*zài . . . xiàmiàn*	在…下面
underground (adj)	*dìxià*	地下
underpass	*dìxià tōngdào*	地下通道
understand	*dǒng*	懂
underwear	*nèiyī*	内衣
uniform	*zhìfú*	制服
unit (organization)	*dānwèi*	单位
united	*liánhé*	联合
United Nations	*Liánhéguó*	联合国
United States	*Měiguó*	美国
university	*dàxué*	大学
until	*dào . . . wéizhǐ*	到…为止
up	*shàng*	上
upstairs	*lóushàng*	楼上
urban	*chéngshì*	城市
urinate	*xiǎobiàn*	小便
US dollar	*měiyuán*	美元
use (n)	*zuòyòng*	作用
use (v)	*yòng*	用
useful	*yǒu yòng*	有用
usually	*tōngcháng , jīngcháng*	通常,经常
vacation (n)	*jiàqī , jià*	假期,假
vacation, spend a	*dùjià*	度假
vaccination	*fángyì zhèng*	防疫证
certificate		
vacuum cleaner	*xīchén qì*	吸尘器
vague	*mōhu*	模糊
valley	*shāngǔ*	山谷
valuable object	*guìzhòng wùpǐn*	贵重物品
value (n)	*jiàzhí*	价值
van (mini-bus)	*miànbāochē*	面包车
Vancouver	*Wēngēhuá*	温哥华
vase	*huāpíng*	花瓶
vegetable	*shūcài*	蔬菜
vegetarian food	*sùshí*	素食
ventilation	*tōngfēng*	通风

vermicelli (dried)	*guàmiàn*	挂面
vertical flute (bamboo)	*xiāo*	箫
very	*hěn*	很
vest	*bèixīn*	背心
vice-president (national)	*fù zǒngtǒng*	副总统
video camera	*shèxiàng jī*	摄像机
video cassette recorder	*lùxiàng jī*	录像机
videotape	*lùxiàng cídài*	录像磁带
Vietnam	*Yuènán*	越南
view (scenery)	*jǐngsè*	景色
viewfinder	*qǔjǐngqì*	取景器
village	*cūnzhuāng*	村庄
village fair	*jíshì*	集市
villain	*ègùn*	恶棍
vinegar	*cù*	醋
violin	*xiǎotíqín*	小提琴
visa	*qiānzhèng*	签证
visa office (PSB)	*gōng'ānjú wàiguǎnchù*	公安局外管处
visit	*cānguān, fǎngwèn*	参观,访问
visit relatives	*tànqīn*	探亲
vocabulary	*cíhuì liàng*	词汇量
vodka	*fútèjiā*	伏特加
voice (n)	*sǎngzi*	嗓子
volleyball	*páiqiú*	排球
voltage	*diànyā*	电压
voltage converter	*biànyāqì*	变压器
volts, 110	*yìbǎi yīshí fú*	110伏
volts, 220	*èrbǎi èrshí fú*	220伏
volume (book)	*juàn*	卷
volume (sound)	*yīnliàng*	音量
vomit	*ǒutù*	呕吐
wage (salary)	*gōngzī*	工资
waist	*yāo*	腰
waist drum	*yāogǔ*	腰鼓
wait	*děng*	等
waiter or waitress	*fúwùyuán*	服务员
waiting lounge	*hòukè shì*	候客室
wake up (self)	*xǐnglái*	醒来

DICTIONARY

wake up (someone else)	*jiàoxǐng*	叫醒
walk	*zǒu , sànbù*	走, 散步
Walkman (personal stereo)	*dānfàng jī*	单放机
wall	*qiáng*	墙
wallet	*píjiāzi*	皮夹子
walnut	*hétao*	核桃
waltz (dance)	*huá'ěrzi*	华尔兹
waltz (music)	*yuánwǔqǔ*	圆舞曲
want (v)	*yào*	要
war	*zhànzhēng*	战争
warm (adj)	*nuǎnhe*	暖和
warm (personality)	*rèqíng*	热情
wash (v)	*xǐ*	洗
washcloth	*xǐliǎn jīn*	洗脸巾
Washington DC	*Huáshèngdùn Tèqū*	华盛顿特区
waste (v)	*làngfèi*	浪费
wastebasket	*zhǐlǒu*	纸篓
watch (v)	*kàn*	看
watch (wristwatch)	*shǒubiǎo*	手表
watchband	*biǎodài*	表带
water (n)	*shuǐ*	水
water caltrop	*língjiǎo*	菱角
water chestnut	*bíqì*	荸荠
water lily	*shuǐfúlián*	水浮莲
water polo	*shuǐqiú*	水球
water-skiing	*huáshuǐ yùndòng*	划水运动
watercolors	*shuǐcǎi*	水彩
waterfall	*pùbù*	瀑布
watermelon	*xīguā*	西瓜
wavy	*bōlàngshì*	波浪式
way (direction)	*fāngxiàng*	方向
way (method)	*fāngfǎ*	方法
we	*wǒmen*	我们
weak	*ruò*	弱
wealth	*cáifù*	财富
wealth (symbol)	*lù*	禄
wear	*chuān , dài*	穿, 戴
weasel	*huángshǔláng*	黄鼠狼
weather	*tiānqì*	天气
weather forecast	*tiānqì yùbào*	天气预报

weave	*biānzhī*	编织
weaving (n)	*zhīpǐn*	织品
wedding	*hūnlǐ*	婚礼
Wednesday	*xīngqī sān*	星期三
week	*xīngqī*	星期
weekend	*zhōumò*	周末
weekly (magazine)	*zhōubào*	周报
weight-lifting	*jǔzhòng*	举重
welcome	*huānyíng*	欢迎
well (adv)	*hǎo*	好
well (n)	*jǐng*	井
west	*xī*	西
West Lake	*Xīhú*	西湖
Western meal	*xīcān*	西餐
Western menu	*xīcān càipǔ*	西餐菜谱
Western toilet	*zuòshì cèsuǒ*	坐式厕所
wet (adj)	*shī*	湿
what	*shénme*	什么
wheat	*màizi*	麦子
wheel	*lúnzi*	轮子
wheelchair	*lúnyǐ*	轮椅
when	*shénme shíhou*	什么时候
where	*nǎli , nǎr*	哪里,哪儿
which	*nǎge , něige*	哪个
whiskey	*wēishìjì*	威士忌
white	*bái*	白
White Peony tea	*Shòuméi chá*	寿眉茶
white edible fungus	*yín' ěr*	银耳
white liquor, Chinese	*báijiǔ*	白酒
white wine	*bái pútáo jiǔ*	白葡萄酒
who (question)	*shéi*	谁
whole	*zhěnggè*	整个
wholeasale	*pīfā*	批发
why	*wèi shénme*	为什么
wide	*kuān*	宽
width	*kuāndù*	宽度
wife	*qīzi , fūrén , àirén*	妻子,夫人,爱人
wildlife preserve	*zìrán bǎohù qū*	自然保护区
will (determination)	*yìzhì*	意志
will (future tense)	*yào*	要
willow tree	*liǔshù*	柳树
win	*yíng*	赢

DICTIONARY

wind (n)	*fēng*	风
wind instrument (music)	*guǎn yuèqì*	管乐器
window	*chuānghu*	窗户
windshield	*dǎngfēng bōli*	挡风玻璃
windsurfing	*fānbǎn yùndòng*	帆板运动
windy	*yǒufēng*	有风
wine	*pútáo jiǔ*	葡萄酒
wine glass	*jiǔbēi*	酒杯
winter	*dōngtiān*	冬天
winter melon	*dōngguā*	冬瓜
wipe	*cā*	擦
wish (n)	*yuànwàng*	愿望
wishing you...	*zhù nǐ...*	祝你……
within	*zài... yǐnèi*	在…以内
wok	*chǎocài guō*	炒菜锅
woman	*fùnǚ*	妇女
women's bike	*nǚchē*	女车
wonderful	*fēicháng jīngcǎi*	非常精彩
wonton	*húndùn*	馄饨
wood	*mùtou*	木头
woodcut	*mùbǎn huà*	木版画
wool	*yángmáo*	羊毛
word	*zì*	字
work (art, literature)	*zuòpǐn*	作品
work (job)	*gōngzuò*	工作
work quota	*gōngzuò liàng*	工作量
work unit	*dānwèi*	单位
worker	*gōngrén*	工人
worker's cap	*yāshémào*	鸭舌帽
workshop	*chējiān*	车间
world	*shìjiè*	世界
World War II	*èr cì dàzhàn*	二次大战
worry	*dānxīn*	担心
worse	*gènghuài, gèngzāo*	更坏,更糟
would like to	*xiǎng*	想
wound (n)	*shāngkǒu*	伤口
wrap	*bāo*	包
wrapping paper	*bāozhuāng zhǐ*	包装纸
wrench (hardware)	*bānshou*	扳手
wrestling	*shuāijiāo*	摔跤
wrist	*shǒuwàn*	手腕

write	*xiě*	写
write down	*xiě xià*	写下
writer	*zuòjiā*	作家
writing brush,	*máobǐ*	毛笔
wrong	*cuò le , bú duì*	错了,不对
X-ray	*X-guāng*	X光
Xerox	*fùyìn*	复印
(see duplication)		
yak	*máoniú*	牦牛
Yangtze River	*Chángjiāng*	长江
yard (3 feet)	*mǎ*	码
year	*nián*	年
years old (age)	*suì*	岁
yellow	*huáng*	黄
yellow croaker	*huánghuāyú*	黄花鱼
Yellow River	*Huánghé*	黄河
Yellow Sea	*Huánghǎi*	黄海
yen	*Rìyuán*	日元
yeasterday	*zuótiān*	昨天
yet	*hái*	还
yogurt	*suānnǎi*	酸奶
you	*nǐ*	你
you (plural)	*nǐmen*	你们
you (polite form)	*nín*	您
young	*niánqīng , xiǎo*	年轻,小
young man	*xiǎo huǒzi*	小伙子
young people	*qīngnián*	青年
young woman	*niánqīng nǔrén*	年轻女人
your	*nǐde*	你的
your (plural)	*nǐmende*	你们的
yurt	*měnggǔbāo*	蒙古包
zebra crosswalk	*bānmǎ xiàn*	斑马线
zero	*líng*	零
zipper	*lāliàn*	拉链
zither, 25-string	*sè*	瑟
zither, 7-string	*gǔqín*	古琴
zither, many-stringed	*zhēng*	筝
zoo	*dòngwùyuán*	动物园

Chinese-English Supplement

This supplement provides English definitions of Chinese terms which are likely to be mentioned to the traveler. In particular, attention has been given to medical vocabulary, names of Chinese foods and products, and words which the traveler might hear in reply to the question *zhèige shì shénme*? (What is this?)

阿斯匹林	*āsīpǐlín*	aspirin
阿姨	*āyí*	auntie
艾滋病	*àizībìng*	AIDS
鹌鹑	*ānchún*	quail
安眠药	*ānmián yào*	sleeping pill
按摩	*ànmó*	massage
八宝饭	*bābǎofàn*	eight precious rice
拔丝苹果	*básī píngguǒ*	honey crystalized apples
拔牙	*báyá*	extract a tooth
白菜	*báicài*	bok choy; cabbage
白果	*báiguǒ*	ginkgo
白酒	*báijiǔ*	Chinese white liquor
白杨树	*báiyángshù*	aspen tree
百	*bǎi*	hundred
百货商店	*bǎihuò shāngdiàn*	department store
柏树	*bǎishù*	cypress tree
斑疹伤寒	*bānzhěn shānghán*	typhus
版画	*bǎnhuà*	print
包车	*bāochē*	hired car
包子	*bāozi*	steamed dumpling
鲍鱼	*bàoyú*	abalone
悲剧	*bēijù*	tragedy
荸荠	*bíqì*	water chestnut
鼻通	*bítōng*	decongestant
鼻子	*bízi*	nose
闭路电视	*bìlù diànshì*	cable TV
避孕用品	*bìyùn yòng pǐn*	contraceptives
便秘	*biàn mì*	constipation

SUPPLEMENT

宾馆	*bīnguǎn*	guesthouse, hotel
冰球	*bīngqiú*	ice hockey
冰糖葫芦	*bīngtáng húlu*	candied haws
丙纶	*bǐnglún*	acrylic
菠菜	*bōcài*	spinach
菠萝	*bōluó*	pineapple
不锈钢	*búxiùgāng*	stainless steel
补牙	*bǔyá*	fill a tooth
菜豆	*càidòu*	kidney bean
菜花	*càihuā*	cauliflower
菜心	*càixīn*	cabbage heart
餐厅	*cāntīng*	dining room, restaurant
蚕	*cán*	silkworm
蚕豆	*cándòu*	broad bean
草药	*cǎoyào*	herbal medicine
侧肋	*cèlèi*	side
厕所	*cèsuǒ*	toilet
叉烧包	*chāshāo bāo*	roast pork bun
茶花	*cháhuā*	camelia
产科病房	*chǎnkē bìngfáng*	maternity ward
长寿	*chángshòu*	longevity
肠子	*chángzi*	bowels
车间	*chējiān*	workshop
城门	*chéngmén*	city gate
城墙	*chéngqiáng*	city wall
成语	*chéngyǔ*	idiom
抽筋	*chōujīn*	cramp
出口货	*chūkǒu huò*	export goods
出血	*chūxuè*	hemorrhage
传染	*chuánrǎn*	infection
船闸	*chuánzhá*	ship lock
春节	*chūnjié*	Chinese New Year
春卷	*chūnjuǎn*	spring roll
葱	*cōng*	scallion
葱头	*cōngtóu*	onion
醋	*cù*	vinegar
催吐剂	*cuītùjì*	emetic
大白菜	*dà báicài*	Chinese cabbage
大便	*dàbiàn*	bowel movement

大理石	dàlǐshí	marble
大麦	dàmài	barley
大虾	dàxiā	prawn
丹顶鹤	dāndǐnghè	red-crowned crane
单位	dānwèi	work unit; organization
单行线	dānxíng xiàn	one-way street
单元	dānyuán	housing unit; doorway
蛋花汤	dànhuātāng	egg-drop soup
刀豆	dāodòu	sword bean
登机牌	dēngjīpái	boarding pass
登记处	dēngjì chù	registration desk
低	dī	low
笛子	dízi	bamboo flute
地铁	dìtiě	subway
点穴法	diǎnxuèfǎ	acupressure
电报	diànbào	telegram
电报挂号	diànbào guàhào	cable address
电传	diànchuán	telex
电传挂号	diànchuán guàhào	telex call number
电疗	diànliáo	electrotherapy
貂	diāo	marten
丁香	dīngxiāng	lilac
丁香酒	dīngxiāng jiǔ	clove wine
丁字路口	dīngzì lùkǒu	T-intersection
定额	dìng' é	quota
冬菇	dōnggū	black mushroom
冬瓜	dōngguā	winter melon
豆瓣酱	dòubàn jiàng	hot bean sauce
豆腐	dòufu	beancurd
豆腐干	dòufu gān	dried beancurd
豆浆	dòujiāng	soybean milk
豆沙	dòushā	sweetened bean paste
豆芽	dòuyá	bean sprout
豆子	dòuzi	bean
杜鹃花	dùjuānhuā	azalea
对	duì	correct
对不起	duìbuqǐ	excuse me, sorry
恶心	ěxīn	nauseous
儿科	érkē	pediatrics department
耳鼻喉科	ěr-bí-hóu kē	ear-nose-throat

SUPPLEMENT

二胡	**èrhú**	department 2-string fiddle
发抖	**fādǒu**	shiver
发炎	**fāyán**	inflammation, infection
蕃茄	**fānqié**	tomato
饭	**fàn**	rice
饭店	**fàndiàn**	hotel; restaurant
饭馆	**fànguǎn**	restaurant
饭后	**fànhòu**	after meals
饭前	**fànqián**	before meals
防疫证	**fángyì zhèng**	vaccination certificate
放射科	**fàngshèkē**	radiology department
翡翠	**fěicuì**	chrysolite
肺	**fèi**	lung
肺结核	**fèi jiéhé**	tuberculosis
肺炎	**fèiyán**	pneumonia
坟墓	**fénmù**	tomb
风湿病	**fēngshī bìng**	rheumatism
凤仙花	**fèngxiānhuā**	touch-me-not
佛经	**fójīng**	sutra
福	**fú**	symbol for luck
服务费	**fúwùfèi**	service fee
服务员	**fúwùyuán**	service attendant
服装店	**fúzhuāng diàn**	clothing store
妇科	**fùkē**	gynecology department
副食品	**fùshí pǐn**	nonstaple food
腹泻	**fùxiè**	diarrhea
复制品	**fùzhìpǐn**	reproduction
芥菜	**gàicài**	leaf mustard
芥蓝	**gàilán**	Chinese broccoli
肝	**gān**	liver
干咸鱼	**gān xián yú**	dried minced fish
干杯!	**Gānbēi!**	Cheers!
干贝	**gānbèi**	scallop
肝炎	**gānyán**	hepatitis
柑子	**gānzi**	mandarin orange
橄榄	**gǎnlǎn**	olive
高	**gāo**	high
高尔夫	**gāo' ěrfū**	golf
高粱	**gāoliáng**	sorghum
膏药	**gāoyào**	medicated plaster

高原	*gāoyuán*	highland
鸽子	*gēzi*	pigeon
隔离病房	*gélí bìngfáng*	isolation ward
蛤蜊	*géli*	clams
公安局	*gōng'ānjú*	Public Security Bureau
公斤	*gōngjīn*	kilogram
公里	*gōnglǐ*	kilometer
公路	*gōnglù*	highway
公顷	*gōngqǐng*	hectare
工艺美术	*gōngyì měishù*	arts and crafts
公寓	*gōngyù*	apartment
工资	*gōngzī*	slary
工作量	*gōngzuò liàng*	work quota
鼓楼	*gǔlóu*	drum tower
古琴	*gǔqín*	7-string zither
骨头	*gǔtou*	bone
挂面	*guàmiàn*	vermicelli
观察室	*guānchá shì*	observation ward
关节	*guānjié*	joints
关节炎	*guānjié yán*	arthritis
关系	*guānxi*	connection, relation
规定	*guīdìng*	regulation
桂花	*guìhuā*	cassia
桂花酒	*guìhuā jiǔ*	cassia wine
锅贴	*guōtiē*	fried dumplings
国画	*guóhuà*	traditional Chinese painting
国务院	*guówùyuàn*	state council
过敏症	*guòmǐn zhèng*	allergy
哈蜜瓜	*hāmìguā*	Hami melon
海关申报单	*hǎiguān shēnbào dān*	customs declaration
海狸	*hǎilí*	beaver
海米	*hǎimǐ*	dried shrimps
海参	*hǎishēn*	sea cucumber
海棠	*hǎitáng*	Chinese crabapple
海鲜	*hǎixiān*	seafood
海蜇	*hàizhé*	jellyfish
含片	*hánpiàn*	throat lozenges
汗	*hàn*	sweat
蚝	*háo*	oyster

SUPPLEMENT

蚝油	*háoyóu*	oyster sauce
好莱坞	*Hǎoláiwū*	Hollywood
荷花	*héhuā*	lotus
核桃	*hétao*	walnut
鹤	*hè*	crane
红茶	*hóngchá*	black tea
红绿灯	*hónglǜdēng*	traffic light
红烧	*hóngshāo*	braised in brown sauce
红薯	*hóngshǔ*	sweet potato
喉咙	*hóulóng*	throat
忽必烈	*Hūbìliè*	Kublai Khan
沪剧	*hùjù*	Shanghai Opera
护照	*hùzhào*	passport
花菜	*huācài*	cauliflower
花粉热	*huāfěn rè*	hay fever
花卷	*huājuǎn*	steamed twisted roll
花生	*huāshēng*	peanut
华侨	*Huáqiáo*	overseas Chinese
化疗	*huàliáo*	chemotherapy
化纤	*huàxiān*	synthetic
槐树	*huáishù*	locust tree
怀孕	*huáiyùn*	pregnant
磺胺	*huáng'ān*	sulfa
黄豆	*huángdòu*	soybean
黄瓜	*huángguā*	cucumber
黄花鱼	*huánghuāyú*	yellow croaker
黄鼠狼	*huángshǔláng*	weasel
昏迷	*hūnmí*	coma
馄饨	*húndùn*	wonton
火锅	*huǒguō*	hot pot
火腿	*huǒtuǐ*	ham
霍乱	*huòluàn*	cholera
机场费	*jīchǎng fèi*	airport departure tax
鸡冠花	*jīguānhuā*	cock's comb
肌肉	*jīròu*	muscle
急救站	*jíjiù zhàn*	first-aid station
集市	*jíshì*	village fair
集邮	*jíyóu*	stamp collecting
急诊室	*jízhěn shì*	emergency room
脊椎	*jǐzhuī*	spine

家乡	jiāxiāng	native place
夹竹桃	jiāzhútáo	oleander
驾驶执照	jiàshǐ zhízhào	driver's license
煎饼	jiānbǐng	crepe, egg pancake
减价	jiǎnjià	price reduction
简谱	jiǎnpǔ	numbered music notation
检疫	jiǎnyì	quarantine
健康表	jiànkāng biǎo	health declaration
健美操	jiànměi cāo	aerobics
江豆	jiāngdòu	green long bean
奖金	jiǎngjīn	bonus
酱油	jiàngyóu	soy sauce
饺子	jiǎozi	boiled dumplings, ravioli
节目	jiémù	program; event
结帐	jiézhàng	settle the bill
借光	jièguāng	excuse me, make way
芥末	jièmo	mustard
筋	jīn	tendon
金桔	jīnjú	kumquat
金丝猴	jīnsīhóu	golden-haired monkey
金鱼	jīnyú	goldfish
金针	jīnzhēn	day-lily bud
进口货	jìnkǒu huò	import goods
京胡	jīnghú	Beijing opera fiddle
经济日报	Jīngjì Rìbào	Economic Daily
京剧	jīngjù	Beijing Opera
痉挛	jìngluán	convulsion
精神病	jīngshénbìng	psychosis
精神分裂	jīngshén fēnliè	schizophrenia
静脉注射	jìngmài zhùshè	intravenous injection
酒	jiǔ	alcoholic beverage
韭菜	jiǔcài	Chinese chives
酒精	jiǔjīng	alcohol
居留证	jūliú zhèng	residence permit
局部麻醉	júbù mázuì	local anesthesia
菊花	júhuā	chrysanthemum
剧场	jùchǎng	theater
开水	kāishuǐ	boiled water

SUPPLEMENT

凯乐	*Kǎiyuè*	Hyatt
抗生素	*kàngshēngsù*	antibiotic
咳嗽	*késòu*	cough
口水	*kǒushuǐ*	saliva
苦瓜	*kǔguā*	bitter gourd
奎宁	*kuíníng*	quinine
溃疡	*kuìyáng*	ulcer
昆曲	*kūnqǔ*	Kunshan Opera
拉肚子	*lā dùzi*	diarrhea
辣酱	*làjiàng*	hot sauce
辣椒	*làjiāo*	chilli pepper
腊梅	*làméi*	allspice
腊肉	*làròu*	dried minced meat
兰花	*lánhuā*	orchid
篮球	*lánqiú*	basketball
劳驾	*láojia*	excuse me, make way
老家	*lǎojiā*	ancestral place
肋骨	*lèigǔ*	rib
梨	*lí*	pear
理发店	*lǐfà diàn*	barbershop
李子	*lǐzi*	plum
痢疾	*lìji*	dysentery
荔枝	*lìzhī*	lychee
栗子	*lìzi*	chestnut
莲花	*liánhuā*	lotus
莲子	*liánzǐ*	lotus seed
烈士	*lièshì*	martyr
菱角	*língjiǎo*	water caltrop
零钱	*língqián*	coins, small bills
零售	*língshòu*	retail
流感	*liúgǎn*	flu
柳树	*liǔshù*	willow tree
龙井茶	*Lóngjīng chá*	Dragon Well tea
龙虾	*lóngxiā*	lobster
龙眼	*lóngyǎn*	longan fruit
禄	*lù*	symbol for wealth
鹿	*lù*	deer
路口	*lùkǒu*	intersection, crossroad
鹿茸	*lùróng*	pilose antler
旅馆	*lǚguǎn*	hotel
旅社	*lǚshè*	hostel

旅行社	*lǚxíngshè*	travel service
绿茶	*lùchá*	green tea
绿豆	*lùdòu*	mung bean
萝卜	*luóbo*	turnip
麻花	*máhuā*	fried dough twists
麻将	*májiàng*	mah-jongg
麻油	*máyóu*	sesame oil
麻疹	*mázhěn*	measles
麻醉	*mázuì*	anesthesia
吗啡	*mǎfēi*	morphine
马克·波罗	*Mǎkě Bōluó*	Marco Polo
玛瑙	*mǎnǎo*	agate
脉搏	*màibó*	pulse
麦子	*màizi*	wheat
馒头	*mántou*	steamed bread
慢车	*mànchē*	local bus or train
慢性	*mànxìng*	chronic
芒果	*mángguǒ*	mango
牦牛	*máoniú*	yak
茅台	*máotái*	Maotai liquor
玫瑰花	*méiguihuā*	rose
梅花	*méihuā*	plum blossom
米	*mǐ*	meter
米老鼠	*Mǐlǎoshǔ*	Mickey Mouse
棉	*mián*	cotton
免费	*miǎnfèi*	free of charge
面条	*miàntiáo*	noodles
蘑菇	*mógu*	mushroom
墨	*mò*	ink stick
末班车	*mò bān chē*	last bus or train
墨斗鱼	*mòdǒuyú*	cuttlefish
茉莉花茶	*mòlì huāchá*	jasmine tea
牡丹	*mǔdān*	peony
墓地	*mùdì*	burial grounds
男厕	*náncè*	men's room
脑膜炎	*nǎomó yán*	meningitis
脑炎	*nǎoyán*	encephalitis
年糕	*niángāo*	glutinous rice cake
年画	*niánhuà*	New Year painting
牛肉	*niúròu*	beef

SUPPLEMENT

女厕	*nǚcè*	women's room
疟疾	*nüèji*	malaria
藕	*ǒu*	lotus root
呕吐	*ǒutù*	vomit
排骨	*páigǔ*	sparerib
牌楼	*páilóu*	memorial arch
排球	*páiqiú*	volleyball
派出所	*pàichūsuǒ*	police station
盘尼西林	*pánníxīlín*	penicillin
螃蟹	*pángxiè*	crab
泡菜	*pàocài*	pickled vegetables
盆地	*péndì*	land basin
盆景	*pénjǐng*	bonsai
朋友	*péngyǒu*	friend
批发	*pīfā*	wholesale
霹雳舞	*pīlìwǔ*	breakdancing
皮蛋	*pídàn*	thousand-year egg
皮肤科	*pífūkē*	dermatology department
琵琶	*pípá*	4-string lute
枇杷	*pípá*	loquat
皮下	*píxià*	hypodermic
皮鞋	*píxié*	leather shoes
皮影	*píyǐng*	shadow puppet
皮疹	*pízhěn*	rash
贫血症	*pínxuě zhèng*	anemia
评剧	*píngjù*	Pingju Opera
平原	*píngyuán*	plains
破伤风	*pò shāngfēng*	tetanus
葡萄	*pútáo*	grape
葡萄干	*pútáo gān*	raisin
葡萄糖	*pútáo táng*	glucose
普洱茶	*pǔ'ěr chá*	Puer tea
普通舱	*pǔtōngcāng*	economy class
祁门红茶	*Qímén hóngchá*	Keemun tea
气喘	*qìchuǎn*	asthma
气功	*qìgōng*	breath energy exercise
千	*qiān*	thousand
千克	*qiānkè*	kilogram

签证	qiānzhèng	visa
蔷薇	qiángwēi	hedge rose
茄子	qiézi	eggplant
芹菜	qíncài	celery
青光眼	qīngguāng yǎn	glaucoma
青椒	qīngjiāo	green pepper
青稞	qīngkē	barley
青霉素	qīngméisù	pencillin
青蛙	qīngwā	frog
清真	qīngzhēn	Moslem
晴纶	qínglún	polyester
秋海棠	qiūhǎitáng	begonia
全身麻醉	quánshēn mázuì	general anesthesia
人民日报	*Rénmín Rìbào*	People's Daily
人参	rénshēn	ginseng
人造丝	rénzào sī	rayon
日报	rìbào	daily newspaper
榕树	róngshù	banyan tree
肉松	ròusōng	shredded dried meat
乳猪	rǔzhū	roast suckling pig
阮	ruǎn	Chinese banjo
软膏	ruǎngāo	ointment
软卧	ruǎnwò	soft-sleeper
软席	ruǎnxí	soft-seat
三弦琴	sānxián qín	3-string guitar
桑树	sāngshù	mulberry tree
嗓子	sǎngzi	throat; voice
瑟	sè	25-string zither
山羊	shānyáng	goat
山芋	shānyù	sweet potato
山楂	shānzhā	haw
鳝鱼	shànyú	eel
商店	shāngdiàn	shop
伤寒	shānghán	typhoid
伤口	shāngkǒu	wound (n)
烧饼	shāobǐng	sesame biscuit
蛇	shé	snake
猞猁	shēlì	lynx
神经病学	shénjīngbìng xué	neurology
神经质	shénjīngzhì	neurosis

SUPPLEMENT

肾	*shèn*	kidney
升	*shēng*	liter
笙	*shēng*	Chinese mouth organ
生姜	*shēngjiāng*	ginger
省	*shěng*	province
师傅	*shīfu*	master worker
失眠	*shīmián*	insomnia
石版画	*shíbǎnhuā*	lithograph
实际	*shíjì*	practical, realistic
石榴	*shíliu*	pomegranate
食品店	*shípǐn diàn*	grocery store
食物中毒	*shíwù zhòng dú*	food poisoning
柿子	*shìzi*	persimmon
收款处	*shōukuǎnchù*	cashier's booth
首班车	*shǒu bān chē*	first bus or train
手风琴	*shǒufēngqín*	accordion
手术室	*shǒushù shì*	operation room
寿	*shòu*	symbol for longevity
寿眉茶	*Shòuméi chá*	White Peony tea
售票处	*shòupiào chù*	ticket office
书店	*shūdiàn*	bookstore
书记处	*shūjìchù*	secretariat
叔叔	*shūshu*	uncle
涮羊肉	*shuànyángròu*	Mongolian hot pot
水貂	*shuǐdiāo*	mink
水浮莲	*shuǐfúlián*	water lily
水饺	*shuǐjiǎo*	ravioli, boiled dumplings
水獭	*shuǐtǎ*	otter
水仙	*shuǐxiān*	narcissus
税	*shuì*	tax
睡前	*shuìqián*	before sleep
四合院	*sìhéyuàn*	traditional Chinese courtyard
四季豆	*sìjìdòu*	string bean
松	*sōng*	pine tree
松花蛋	*sōnghuādàn*	thousand-year egg
宿舍	*sùshè*	dormitory; housing
酸	*suān*	sore; sour
酸辣汤	*suānlà tāng*	hot-and-sour soup
酸奶	*suānnǎi*	yogurt

蒜	*suàn*	garlic
孙中山	*Sūn Zhōngshān*	Sun Yat-sen
唢呐	*suǒnà*	Chinese cornet
台风	*táifēng*	typhoon
太监	*tàijiān*	eunuch
滩羊	*tānyáng*	argali sheep
汤	*tāng*	soup
汤面	*tāngmiàn*	soup noodles
唐老鸭	*Tánglǎoyā*	Donald Duck
糖尿病	*tángniàobìng*	diabetes
桃子	*táozi*	peach
特快	*tèkuài*	express
疼	*téng*	pain
体温	*tǐwēn*	temperature
体育馆	*tǐyùguǎn*	gymnasium
甜菜	*tiáncài*	beet
铁观音茶	*Tiěguānyīn chá*	Iron Goddess of Mercy tea
同志	*tóngzhì*	comrade
痛苦	*tòngkǔ*	pain
头班车	*tóu bān chē*	first bus or train
头等舱	*tóuděngcāng*	first class
头晕	*tóuyūn*	dizzy
兔子	*tùzi*	rabbit
推拿	*tuīná*	massage
退热	*tuìrè*	antipyretic
吞咽	*tūnyàn*	swallow
外宾	*wàibīn*	foreign guest
外汇	*wàihuì*	foreign exchange certificate
外科	*wàikē*	surgery department
外用	*wàiyòng*	external use
豌豆黄	*wāndòu huáng*	pea-flour cake
万	*wàn*	ten thousand
危急	*wēijí*	critical
围棋	*wéiqí*	go
胃穿孔	*wèi chuānkǒng*	gastric perforation
胃疼	*wèiténg*	stomachache
胃炎	*wèiyán*	gastritis

SUPPLEMENT

蚊子	*wénzi*	mosquito
问讯处	*wènxún chù*	information desk
莴笋	*wōsǔn*	asparagus lettuce
乌龟	*wūguī*	tortoise
乌龙茶	*wūlóng chá*	oolong tea
乌贼	*wūzéi*	cuttlefish
无轨电车	*wúguǐ diànchē*	trolley
无花果	*wúhuāguǒ*	fig
梧桐树	*wútóngshù*	Chinese parasol tree
五粮液	*wǔliángyè*	five-grain liquor
武术	*wǔshù*	martial arts
舞厅	*wǔtīng*	dance hall
五线谱	*wǔxiàn pǔ*	5-line musical staff
希尔顿	*Xī'ěrdùn*	Hilton
西餐	*xīcān*	Western meal
稀饭	*xīfàn*	porridge, congee
西红柿	*xīhóngshì*	tomato
喜	*xǐ*	symbol for happiness
囍	*xǐ*	double happiness
喜来登	*Xǐláidēng*	Sheraton
喜玛拉雅山	*Xǐmǎlāyǎ shān*	Himalayas
虾	*xiā*	shrimp
咸鸭蛋	*xián yādàn*	salted duck egg
衔接航班	*xiánjiē hángbān*	connecting flight
县	*xiàn*	county
乡	*xiāng*	township
香菜	*xiāngcài*	coriander
香格里拉	*Xiānggélǐlā*	Shangri-La
香菇	*xiānggū*	black mushroom
香酥鸡	*xiāngsū jī*	fried crisp chicken
香酥鸭	*xiāngsū yā*	crispy duck
香油	*xiāngyóu*	sesame oil
香肠	*xiāngcháng*	sausage
象棋	*xiàngqí*	Chinese chess
相声	*xiàngsheng*	cross talk
箫	*xiāo*	vertical bamboo flute
消毒膏	*xiāodú gāo*	antiseptic cream
消化	*xiāohuà*	digestion
小笼包	*xiǎolóng bāo*	small steamed dumpling
小山羊皮	*xiǎoshānyáng pí*	kidskin

小熊猫	*xiǎoxióngmāo*	lesser panda
小羊皮	*xiǎoyáng pí*	lambskin
泻药	*xièyào*	cathartic
新石器时代	*xīn shíqì shídài*	Neolithic era
心绞痛	*xīnjiǎotòng*	angina pectoris
心理学	*xīnlǐxué*	psychology
心力衰竭	*xīnlì shuāijié*	cardiac failure
心跳	*xīntiào*	palpitation
心脏病发作	*xīnzàngbìng fāzuò*	heart attack
猩红热	*xīnghóngrè*	scarlet fever
杏	*xìng*	apricot
幸福	*xìngfú*	happiness
杏仁	*xìngrén*	almond
杏仁茶	*xìngrénchá*	almond-flour tea
杏仁豆腐	*xìngrén dòufu*	almond gelatin
休克	*xiūkè*	shock
绣球	*xiùqiú*	geranium
岫玉	*xiùyù*	Manchurian jasper
宣纸	*xuānzhǐ*	rice paper
血	*xuè*	blood
血压	*xuèyā*	blood pressure
血型	*xuèxíng*	blood type
熏鱼	*xūnyú*	smoked fish
牙科医生	*yákē yīshēng*	dentist
亚麻布	*yàmá bù*	linen
腌黄瓜	*yān huánggua*	pickled cucumber
阉鸡	*yānjī*	capon
研究所	*yánjiūsuǒ*	research institute; graduate school
岩溶	*yánróng*	karst
眼科	*yǎnkē*	opthamology department
眼药水	*yǎnyàoshuǐ*	eye drops
咽	*yàn*	swallow
砚台	*yàntai*	ink slab
羊毛	*yángmáo*	wool
杨梅	*yángméi*	red bayberry
扬琴	*yángqín*	dulcimer
羊肉	*yángròu*	mutton
痒	*yǎng*	itch

SUPPLEMENT

氧气	*yǎngqì*	oxygen
样品	*yàngpǐn*	sample
腰鼓	*yāogǔ*	waist drum
腰果	*yāoguǒ*	cashew nut
腰疼	*yāoténg*	lumbago
药	*yào*	medicine
药方	*yàofāng*	prescription
药房	*yàofáng*	pharmacy
药丸	*yàowán*	pill
椰子	*yēzi*	coconut
夜班车	*yèbān chē*	night bus
腋下	*yèxià*	underarm
亿	*yì*	hundred million
译制片	*yìzhì piàn*	dubbed film
音乐厅	*yīnyuè tīng*	concert hall
银耳	*yín'ěr*	white edible fungus
银杏	*yínxìng*	ginkgo
饮料	*yǐnliào*	beverage
印泥	*yìnní*	red paste for seals
英里	*yīnglǐ*	mile
樱桃	*yīngtáo*	cherry
硬卧	*yìngwò*	hard-sleeper
硬坐	*yìngzuò*	hard-seat
油菜	*yóucài*	rape
邮局	*yóujú*	post office
邮票	*yóupiào*	postage stamp
油条	*yóutiáo*	fried cruller
鱿鱼	*yóuyú*	squid
柚子	*yòuzi*	pomelo
鱼	*yú*	fish
鱼翅汤	*yúchì tāng*	shark's fin soup
榆树	*yúshù*	elm tree
羽毛球	*yǔmáoqiú*	badminton
豫剧	*yùjù*	Henan Opera
芋头	*yùtou*	taro
鸳鸯	*yuānyang*	mandarin ducks
原作	*yuánzuò*	original
月季	*yuèjì*	Chinese rose
月经	*yuèjīng*	menstruation
越剧	*yuèjù*	Shaoxing Opera
粤剧	*yuèjù*	Cantonese Opera

月票	*yuèpiào*	monthly ticket
月琴	*yuèqín*	4-string mandolin
芸豆	*yúndòu*	kidney bean
枣	*zǎo*	date
澡堂	*zǎotáng*	bathhouse
榨菜	*zhàcài*	hot pickled mustard tuber
占线	*zhànxiàn*	busy line
樟树	*zhāngshù*	camphor tree
招待所	*zhāodàisuǒ*	guesthouse
针灸	*zhēnjiǔ*	acupuncture
真丝	*zhēnsī*	silk
珍珠	*zhēnzhū*	pearl
诊断	*zhěnduàn*	diagnosis
镇	*zhèn*	town
镇静剂	*zhènjìngjì*	tranquilizer
筝	*zhēng*	many-stringed zither
政治局	*zhèngzhìjú*	political bureau
症状	*zhèngzhuàng*	symptom
支气管炎	*zhīqìguǎn yán*	bronchitis
止疼药	*zhǐténg yào*	pain-killer
中餐	*zhōngcān*	Chinese meal
钟楼	*zhōnglóu*	bell tower
中药	*zhōngyào*	traditional Chinese medicine
肿胀	*zhǒngzhàng*	swelling
中暑	*zhòngshǔ*	sunstroke
粥	*zhōu*	porridge, congee
珠穆朗玛峰	***Zhūmùlángmǎ fēng***	Mount Everest
猪肉	*zhūròu*	pork
竹笋	*zhúsǔn*	bamboo shoot
注射	*zhùshè*	injection
住院处	*zhùyuàn chù*	inpatient department
紫貂	*zǐdiāo*	sable
足球	*zúqiú*	soccer
钻石	*zuànshí*	diamond

Numbers and Quantities

Cardinal Numbers

Numeral			Comments
0	零	*líng*	
1	一	*yī**	*1 is read as *yāo* when stating a phone number, room number, bus number, and such identifications.
2	二	*èr***	
3	三	*sān*	
4	四	*sì*	
5	五	*wǔ*	
6	六	*liù*	**2 is usually read as *liǎng* when referring to quantity. For example, "two people" would be *liǎng gè rén*.
7	七	*qī*	
8	八	*bā*	
9	九	*jiǔ*	
10	十	*shí*	
20	二十	*èrshí*	two tens
30	三十	*sānshí*	three tens
40...	四十	*sìshí*	four tens...
11	十一	*shíyī*	ten and one
12	十二	*shí'èr*	ten and two
13...	十三	*shísān*...	ten and three...
21	二十一	*èrshíyī*	twenty and one
22	二十二	*èrshíèr*	twenty and two
23...	二十三	*èrshísān*...	twenty and three...
100	百	*bǎi*	
1,000	千	*qiān*	
10,000	万	*wàn*	
1,000,000	百万	*bǎiwàn*	

Ordinal Numbers

Ordinal number are formed by inserting *dì* in front of the number.

first	*dìyī*	第一
second	*dì'èr*	第二
third...	*dìsān*	第三
first one	*dìyīgè*	第一个
first time	*dìyīcì*	第一次

Fractions

Except for one-half. *yí bàn*, fractions are formed in the pattern (D) *fēnzhī*(N) with D being the denominator and N the numerator.

Examples:

1/3	*sān fēnzhī yī*	三分之一
1/4	*sì fēnzhī yī*	四分之一
3/4	*sì fēnzhī sān*	四分之三
2/5	*wǔ fēnzhī èr*	五分之二

Percentages

To form a percentage, use the pattern *bǎi fēn zhī* (P) with P being the percentage.

Examples:

25%	*bǎi fēnzhī èrshí wǔ*	百分之二十五
80%	*bǎi fēnzhībāshí*	百分之八十
100%	*bǎi fēnzhī yìbǎi*	百分之一百

Measure Words

Measure Word		What It Modifies	Examples
bǎ	把	knives, chairs, keys	*sān bǎ dāo* (3 knives) *yì bǎ yǐzi* (a chair)
běn	本	books	*yì běn xiǎoshuō* (a novel) *liǎng běn zìdiǎn* (2 dictionaries)
duì	对	pairs, couples	*yí duì huāpíng* (a pair of vases) *sān duì fūfù* (3 married couples)
fèn	份	portions, printed matter, newspapers	*yí fèn "Zhōngguó Rìbào"* (a copy of China Daily)
fēng	封	letters (mail)	*liǎng fēng xìn* (2 letters)
gè	个	most things	*sān gè rén* (3 people) *yí gè píngguǒ* (an apple) *wǔ gè xīngqī* (5 weeks)
jiān	间	rooms	*liǎng jiān wòshì* (2 bedrooms)
jiàn	件	clothing, suitcases	*yí jiàn chènshān* (a shirt) *liǎng jiàn xíngli* (2 suitcases)
kē	棵	trees	*yì kē sōng shù* (a pine tree)
kuài	块	rectangular objects, money	*yì kuài féizào* (a bar of soap) *sì kuài miànbāo* (4 slices of bread) *shí kuài qián* (10 yuan)

liàng	辆	vehicles	*yí liàng zìxíngchē* (a bicycle) *liǎng liàng qìchē* (2 cars)
pán	盘	flat, circular objects	*zhèi pán cídài* (this tape cassette) *wǔ pán cài* (5 dishes of food)
shuāng	双	pairs related to hands and feet	*yì shuāng píxié* (a pair of leather shoes) *sì shuāng shǒutào* (4 pairs of gloves)
tái	台	machines	*yì tái dǎzìjī* (a type writer) *yì tái jìsuànjī* (a computer)
tiáo	条	long, linear objects	*yì tiáo kùzi* (a pair of pants) *yì tiáo jiē* (a street) *sān tiáo yú* (3 fish)
zhāng	张	sheets, such as paper, tickets, photos, maps	*liǎng zhāng piào* (2 tickets) *jǐ zhāng zhǐ* (some sheets of paper)
zhī	只	animals	*sān zhī niǎo* (3 birds) *yì zhī lǎohǔ* (a tiger)
zhī	支	writing tools	*yì zhī máobǐ* (a Chinese brush) *sān zhī gāngbǐ* (3 fountain pens)

Expressions of Time

Divisions of the Day

morning	*zǎoshang , zǎochén*	早上,早晨
mid-morning	*shàngwǔ*	上午
noon	*zhōngwǔ*	中午
afternoon	*xiàwǔ*	下午
evening	*wǎnshang*	晚上
night	*yèlǐ*	夜里

Hours and Minutes

hour	*xiǎoshí , zhōngtóu*	小时,钟头
half	*bàn*	半
quarter	*kè*	刻
o'clock	*diǎn , diǎnzhōng*	点,点钟
minute	*fēn , fēnzhōng*	分,分钟
less	*chà*	差

Examples:

3 hours	*sān gè xiǎoshí*
3 1/2 hours	*sān gè bàn xiǎoshí*
8:00	*bā diǎn , bā diǎn zhōng*
8:05	*bā diǎn líng wǔ*
8:10	*bā diǎn shí fēn*
8:15	*bā diǎn yí kè*
8:30	*bā diǎn bàn*
8:50	*bā diǎn wǔshí , jiǔ diǎn chā shí fēn*
9:00 am	*zǎoshang jiǔ diǎn*
9:00 pm	*wǎnshang jiǔ diǎn*
2:00 pm	*xiàwǔ liǎng diǎn*
2:00 am	*yèlǐ liǎng diǎn*

Conversion Charts

Measures

The metric system is widely used in China, along with a few traditional Chinese units of measure. The chart below gives rough equivalences among the various systems. The Chinese translations of the metric and American units, such as *shēng* for liter, can be found in the dictionary.

Chinese Unit	Metric Unit	American Unit

Length

	1cm	.4in
	2.5cm	1in
	30.5cm	1ft
1 *chǐ* 尺	33.3cm	13.1in
	91.4cm	1yd
3 *chǐ*	1m	39.4in
1 *lǐ* 里	.5km	.3mi
2 *lǐ*	1km	.6mi
	1.6km	1mi

Area

	6.5 sq cm	1 sq in
	929 sq cm	1 sq ft
	.8 sq m	1 sq yd
	1 sq m	1550 sq in
1 *mǔ* 亩	674.5 sq m	807 sq yd
6 *mǔ*	4,047 sq m	1 acre
15 *mǔ*	1 ha	2.5 acres
	1 sq km	.4 sq mi
	2.6 sq km	1 sq mi

Weight

1 *qián*	钱	5g	.2 oz
		28.4 g	1 0z
1 *liǎng*	两	50g	1.8 oz
		454g	1 lb
1 *jīn*	斤	500g	1.1 lb
2 *jīn*		1kg	2.2 lb
		.9MT	1 ton
2,000 *jīn*		1MT	2,204.6 lb

Capacity

1cl	.3fl oz	1.1 l	1 qt (dry)
47.3 cl	1 pt (fl)	3.8 l	1 gal (fl)
55 cl	1 pt(dry)	8.8 l	1 pk
94.6 cl	1 qt (fl)	35.2 l	1 bu
1 l	1.1 qt (fl)	1 hl	2.8 bu
1 l	.9 qt(dry)		

Temperature

To calculate the Fahrenheit equivalent of a centigrade temperature, use this formula:
$F = 32 + 1.8C$

°C	°F
35	95
30	86
25	77
20	68
15	59
10	50
5	41
0	32
-5	23
-10	14
-15	5
-20	-4

Money

Chinese Currency

The Chinese currency is called *rénmínbì*(RMB), with the basic unit being the *yuán*(¥). One-tenth of a yuan is called a *jiǎo*. One-hundredth of a yuan is called a *fēn*.

In spoken Chinese, a yuan is often called a *kuài* and a jiao is called a *máo*. When stating a price, the last identifying word "mao" or "fen" is left out.

Examples:

¥ 15.00	*shíwǔkuài*
¥ 15.65	*shíwǔkuàiliùmáowǔ* (no"fen")
¥ 1.50	*yíkuàiwǔ* (no "mao")
¥ .30	*sān máo*
¥ .32	*sānmáoèr*(no "fen")
¥ .02	*liǎngfēn*

Foreign Currencies

US dollar	*Měiyuán*	美元
Canadian dollar	*Jiāyuán*	加元
Australian dollar	*Àoyuán*	澳元
New Zealand dollar	*Xīnxīlányuán*	新西兰元
Pound sterling	*Yīngbàng*	英镑
Japanese yen	*Rìyuán*	日元
Hong Kong dollar	*Gǎngbì*	港币
Euro	*Ōuyuán*	欧元

Key Words:

currency	*bì*	币		mark	*mǎkè*	马克
dollar	*yuán*	元		peso	*bǐsuǒ*	比索
franc	*fǎláng*	法郎		pound	*bàng*	镑
lira	*lǐlā*	里拉		rupee	*lúbǐ*	卢比

Place Names

Major Administrative Divisions

China is divided into 23 provinces, 5 autonomous regions, 4 municipalities directly under the Central Government. and 2 special administrative region.

Municipalities under the Central Government

北京	*Běijīng*
上海	*Shànghǎi*
天津	*Tiānjīn*
重庆	*Chóngqìng*

Autonomous Regions

广西	*Guǎngxī* (Zhuang Autonomous Region)
内蒙古	*NèiMěnggǔ* (Inner Mongolia)
宁夏	*Níngxià* (Hui Autonomous Region)
新疆	*Xīnjiāng* (Uygur Autonomous Region)
西藏	*Xīzàng* (Tibet)

Provinces

安徽	*Ānhuī*	江西	*Jiāngxī*
福建	*Fújiàn*	吉林	*Jílín*
甘肃	*Gānsù*	辽宁	*Liáoníng*
广东	*Guǎngdōng*	青海	*Qīnghǎi*
贵州	*Guìzhōu*	山东	*Shāndōng*
海南	*Hǎinán*	山西	*Shānxī*
河北	*Héběi*	陕西	*Shǎnxī*
河南	*Hénán*		(Shaanxi)
黑龙江	*Hēilóngjiāng*	四川	*Sìchuān*
湖北	*Húběi*	台湾	*Táiwān*
湖南	*Húnán*	云南	*Yúnnán*

APPENDIX F

| 江苏 | *Jiāngsū* | 浙江 | *Zhèjiāng* |

Special Administrative Region

| 香港 | *Xiānggǎng* (Hongkong) |
| 澳门 | *Àomén* (Macao) |

Cities of Interest

Below is a selected list of cities with historic, cultural, or economic significance.

鞍山	*Ānshān*	江陵	*Jiānglíng*
包头	*Bāotóu*	景德镇	*Jǐngdézhèn*
保定	*Bǎodìng*	景洪	*Jǐnghóng*
北戴河	*Běidàihé*	喀什	*Kāshí* (Kashgar)
北京	*Běijīng*		
长春	*Chángchūn*	开封	*Kāifēng*
长沙	*Chángshā*	昆明	*Kūnmíng*
承德	*Chéngdé*	拉萨	*Lāsà* (Lhasa)
成都	*Chéngdū*	兰州	*Lánzhōu*
重庆	*Chóngqìng*	洛阳	*Luòyáng*
大理	*Dàlǐ*	南昌	*Nánchāng*
大连	*Dàlián*	南京	*Nánjīng*
大同	*Dàtóng*	南宁	*Nánníng*
大足	*Dàzú*	宁波	*Níngbō*
敦煌	*Dūnhuáng*	青岛	*Qīngdǎo*
佛山	*Fóshān*	曲阜	*Qǔfù*
抚顺	*Fǔshùn*	泉州	*Quánzhōu*
福州	*Fúzhōu*	日喀则	*Rìkezé* (Shigatse, Xigaze)
格尔木	*Gé'ěrmù* (Golmud)		
广州	*Guǎngzhōu* (Canton)	上海	*Shànghǎi*
		韶山	*Sháoshān*
桂林	*Guìlín*	绍兴	*Shàoxīng*
哈尔滨	*Hā'ěr bīn* (harbin)	深圳	*Shēnzhèn*
		沈阳	*Shěnyáng*
海口	*Hǎikǒu*	石家庄	*Shíjiāzhuāng*
杭州	*Hángzhōu*	苏州	*Sūzhōu*

合肥	*Héféi*	太原	*Tàiyuán*
呼和浩特	*Hūhéhàotè*	天津	*Tiānjīn*
	(Hohhot)	吐鲁番	*Tǔlǔfān*
吉林	*jílín*		(Turfan)
济南	*Jǐnán*	温州	*Wēnzhōu*
乌鲁木齐	*Wūlǔmùqí*	延安	*Yán'ān*
	(Urumqi)	扬州	*Yángzhōu*
无锡	*Wúxī*	宜昌	*Yíchāng*
武汉	*Wǔhàn*	岳阳	*Yuèyáng*
西安	*Xī'ān*	肇庆	*Zhàoqìng*
西宁	*Xīníng*	镇江	*Zhènjiāng*
厦门	*Xiàmén*	郑州	*Zhèngzhōu*
	(Amoy)		

APPENDIX G

Dynasties

The Chinese dynasties are outlined here in brief.

Xia 夏		ca 21st—16th cent BC
Shang 商		ca 16th—11th cent BC
Zhou 周		ca 11th cent—221 BC
Western Zhou		
Eastern Zhou		
Spring and Autumn		
Warring States		
Qin 秦		221—207 BC
Han 汉		206 BC—AD 220
Western Han		
Eastern Han		
Three Kingdoms	三国	220—280
Western Jin	西晋	265—316
Eastern Jin	东晋	317—420
Northern and Southern Dynasties	南北朝	420—581
Sui 隋		581—618
Tang 唐		618—907
Five Dynasties	五代	907—960
Song 宋		960—1279
Northern Song		
Southern Song		
Yuan 元		1271—1368
Ming 明		1368—1644
Qing 清		1644—1911

Family Relations

In Chinese, addressing relatives is not just a matter of calling "aunt" or "uncle"—you have to specify whether the relative is on your mother or father's side and sometimes the relative's age in respect to yourself or your parent.

Paternal Relatives

爷爷	*yéye*	grandfather
奶奶	*nǎinai*	grandmother
伯伯	*bóbo*	uncle (father's older brother)
伯母	*bómǔ*	his wife
叔叔	*shūshu*	uncle (father's younger brother)
婶婶	*shěnshen*	his wife
姑姑	*gūgu*	aunt (father's sister)
姑夫	*gūfu*	her husband
堂哥	*táng gē*	older boy cousin
堂弟	*táng dì*	younger boy cousin
堂姐	*táng jiě*	older girl cousin
堂妹	*táng mèi*	younger girl cousin

Maternal Relatives

姥爷,外公	*lǎoye, wàigōng*	grandfather
姥姥,外婆	*lǎolao, wàipó*	grandmother
姨姨	*yíyi*	aunt (mother's sister)
姨夫	*yífu*	her husband
舅舅	*jiùjiu*	uncle (mother's brother)
舅妈	*jiùmā*	his wife
表哥	*biǎogē*	older boy cousin
表弟	*biǎodì*	younger boy cousin
表姐	*biǎojiě*	older girl cousin
表妹	*biǎomèi*	younger girl cousin

continued

Immediate Family

爸爸	**bàba**	father
妈妈	**māma**	mother
哥哥	**gēge**	older brother
嫂子	**sǎozi**	his wife
弟弟	**dìdi**	younger brother
弟妹, 弟媳	**dìmèi, dìxí**	his wife
姐姐	**jiějie**	older sister
姐夫	**jiěfu**	her husband
妹妹	**mèimei**	younger sister
妹夫	**mèifu**	her husband
女儿	**nǚér**	daughter
女婿	**nǚxu**	son-in-law
儿子	**érzi**	son
媳妇	**xífù**	daughter-in-law
孙子	**sūnzi**	grandson (son's son)
孙女	**sūnnǚ**	granddaughter (son's daughter)
外孙	**wàisūn**	grandson (daughter's son)
外孙女	**wàisūnnǚ**	granddaughter (daughter's daughter)

Useful Telephone Numbers

Emergency

Fire: 119
Police: 110
Traffic accident: 122
Ambulance: 120

Telephone

Domestic long distance calls inquires: 116/176
Registration: 113/173
Information: 174
International calls: 115

Others

Telephone number inquiry: 114
Weather forcast: 121/221
Speaking clock: 117

Foreign Embassies in Beijing

Foreign embassies in Beijing are Mainly located in two areas: Jianguomenwai and Sanlitun. A few are in hotels or diplomatic buildings.

Embassies normally work 5 days a week, and have holidays on both Chinese and their own countries' festivals. They open at 9 a.m. and close at 5 p.m. Visa sections usually work in the morning and some may not open in the afternoon, so please check before you go.

Afghanistan
8 Dongzhimenwai St.
Tel: 65321582

Albania
28 Guanghua Rd. Jianguomenwai
Tel: 65321120

Algeria
7 Sanlitun Rd. Sanlitun
Tel: 65321231/65321232

Angola
Diplomatic Building, Tayuan
Tel: 65326908

Argentina
11 Dongwu St., Sanlitun
Tel: 65321406

Australia
21 Dongzhimenwai St., Sanlitun
Tel: 65322331-7
Fax: 65324605

Austria
5 Xiushui South St., Jianguomen wai
Tel: 65322061
Fax: 65321505

Azerbaijan
7-2-5-1 Diplomatic Building, Tayuan
Tel: 65324614

Bahrain
2-9-2 Diplomatic Building, Tayuan
Tel: 65325025

Bangladesh
42 Guanghua Road
Tel: 65322521/65323706

Belarus
5-2-121 Diplomatic Building, Tayuan
Tel: 65326426

Belgium
6 Sanlitun Rd., Sanlitun
Tel: 65321736 / 65321737 / 65321738
Fax: 65323507

Benin
38 Guanghua Rd., Jianguomenwai
Tel: 65322741 / 65322302

Bolivia
2-3-1 Diplomatic Building, Tayuan
Tel: 65323074/ 65324370

Botswana
1-8-1/1-8-2 Diplomatic Building, Tayuan
Tel: 65325751/5

Brazil
27 Guanghua Rd.
Tel: 65322881/ 65323883

Brunei
91-1 Diplomatic Building, Sanlitun
Tel: 65324094/ 65324095

Bulgaria
4 Xiushui North St., Jianguomenwai
Tel: 65321946/65321916

Burundi
25 Guanghua Rd.
Tel: 65322328/65321801

Cambodia
9 Dongzhimenwai St. Sanlitun
Tel: 65321889

Cameroon
7 Dongwu St., Sanlitun
Tel:65321828/ 65321771

Canada
19 Dongzhimenwai St., Sanlitun
Tel: 65323536

Chad
21 Guanghua Rd., Jianguomenwai
Tel:65321296/ 65321925/ 65324830

Chile
1 Dongsijie St., Sanlitun
Tel: 65321641

Colombia
34 Guanghua Rd.
Tel:65323377/ 65323367

The Congo
7 Dongsijie St., Sanlitun
Tel: 65321658/ 65321417

Croatia
2-1-31 Diplomatic Building, Sanlitun
Tel: 65326241/ 65326242/ 65326256

Cuba
1 Xiushui South St., Jianguomenwai
Tel: 65326568

Cyprus
2-13-2 Diplomatic Building, Tayuan
Tel: 65325057

Czech
Ritan Rd., Jianguomenwai
Tel: 65321531
Fax: 65324814

APPENDIX J

Denmark
1 Dongwujie St. , Sanlitun
Tel: 65322431/ 65322423/
65322438

Ecuador
11-21 Diplomatic Building,
Jianguomenwai
Tel: 65323158

Egypt
2 Ritan East Rd. , Jian-
guomenwai
Tel: 65321825/ 65322760

Equatorial Guinea
2 Dongsijie St. , Sanlitun
Tel: 65323679

Eritrea
1-4-2 Diplomatic Building,
Tayuan
Tel: 65326534

Ethiopia
3 Xiushui South St. , Jianguomenwai
Tel: 65325258

Finland
1-10-1 Diplomatic Building,
Tayuan
Tel: 65321817/ 65321806/
65323646
Fax: 65321884

France
3 Dongsanjie St. , Sanlitun
Tel: 65321331/ 65321274

Gabon
36 Guanghua Rd. , Jian-

guomenwai
Tel: 65322810/ 65323824

Germany.
5 Dongzhimenwai St. , Sanlitun
Tel: 65322161-65
Fax: 65325336

Ghana
8 Sanlitun Rd. , Sanlitun
Tel: 65321319/ 65321544/
65322012

Greece
19 Guanhua Rd. , Jian-
guomenwai
Tel: 65321317/ 65321391/
65321588

Guinea
2 Xiliujie St. , Sanlitun
Tel: 65323649

Guyana
1 Xiushui East St. , Jianguomenwai
Tel: 65321337

Hungary
10 Dongzhimenwai St. , Sanlitun
Tel: 65321431/ 65321432/
65321433

India
1 Ritan East Rd. , Jian-
guomenwai
Tel: 65321908/ 65321856
Fax: 65324684

Indonesia

Diplomatic Building, Sanlitun
Tel: 65325488/ 65325489/
65325484

Iran
13 Dongliujie St., Sanlitun
Tel: 65322040/ 65324870/
65324871

Iraq
25 Xiushui North St., Jianguomenwai
Tel: 65323385/ 65321873

Ireland
3 Ritan South Rd., Jian-
guomenwai
Tel: 65322691/ 665322914/
65321144

Israel
Room 405, West Wing,
China World Trade Centre
1 Jiangguomenwai Ave.
Tel: 65052970/ 65052971/
65052972

Italy
2 Dongerijie St., Sanlitun
Tel: 65322131-2-3-4
Fax: 65324676

The Ivory Coast
9 Beixiaojie St., Sanlitun
Tel: 65321482/ 65323572/
65323192

Japan
7 Ritan Rd. Jianguomenwai
Tel: 65322361

Jordan

5 Dongliujie St., Sanlitun
Tel: 65323906/ 65324654

Kazakhstan
1-13-1/1-13-2 Diplomatic Building, Tayuan
Tel: 65326182/ 65326183

Kenya
4 Xiliujie St., Sanlitun
Tel: 65323381/ 65322478

**People's Democratic Repub-
lic of Korea**
Ritan North Rd., Jian-
guomenwai
Tel: 65321186/ 65321193/
65325018

Republic of Korea
Floor 4, China World Trade
Centre
Tel: 65053171/ 65052608/
65052587

Kuwait
23 Guanghua Rd., Jian-
guomenwai
Tel: 65322216/ 65322182/
65322374

Kirghizia
2-4-1 Diplomatic Building,
Tayuan
Tel: 65326458

Laos
11 Dongliujie St., Sanlitun
Tel: 65321224

Lebanon
51 Dongliujie St., Sanlitun

Tel: 65321560/ 65322197/ 65323281

Libya
3 Dongliujie St., Sanlitun
Tel: 65323666

Luxembourg
21 Neiwubu St.
Tel: 65135937

Macedonia
5-2-22 Diplomatic Building, Sanlitun
Tel: 65326282

Madagascar
3 Sanlitun Dongjie St., Sanlitun
Tel: 65321353/ 65321643/ 65322571

Malaysia
13 Dongzhimenwai St.
Tel: 65322531/ 65322532/ 65322533
Fax: 65325032

Mali
8 Dongsijie St., Sanlitun
Tel: 65321704/ 65321687

Malta
2-1-22 Diplomatic Building, Tayuan
Tel: 65323114

Marshall Islands
1-12-2 Diplomatic Building, Tayuan
Tel: 65325819/ 65325904

Mauritania

9 Dongsanjie St., Sanlitun
Tel: 65321346/ 65321703

Mexico
5 Dongwujie St., Sanlitun
Tel: 65322574/ 65322070/ 65322551

Mongolia
2 Xiushui North St., Jianguomenwai
Tel: 65321203/ 65321810/ 65321952

Morocco.
16 Sanlitun Rd., Sanlitun
Tel: 65321796/ 65321439

Mozambique
1-7-1 Diplomatic Building, Tayuan
Tel: 65323664/65323578

Myanmar
6 Dongzhimenwai St.,
Tel: 65321425

Nepal
1 Xiliujie St., Sanlitun
Tel: 65321795

The Netherlands
1-15-2 Diplomatic Building, Tayuan
Tel: 65321131/65321132/ 65321133
Fax:65324689

New Zealand
1 Dong'erjie St., Ritan Rd., Jianguomenwai
Tel: 65322731/65322732/

65322733
Fax: 65324317

Nigeria
1 Dongyijie St., Sanlitun
Tel: 65323631/65323632/
65323633

Norway
1 Dongyijie St., Sanlitun
Tel: 65322261/65321329/
65323113
Fax:65322392

Oman
6 Liangmahe South Rd., Sanlitun
Tel: 65323692/65323276

Pakistan
1 Dongzhimenwai St., Sanlitun
Tel: 65322504/65322695/
65322581

Palestine
2 Dongsanjie St., Sanlitun
Tel: 65321361

Papua New Guinea
2-11-2 Diplomatic Building,
Tayuan
Tel: 65324312/65324709

Peru
2-82 Diplomatic Building, Sanlitun
Tel: 65324658/65323719

The Philippines
23 Xiushui North St., Jianguomenwai

Tel: 65321872/65322518/
65322451

Poland
1 Ritan Rd., Jianguomenwai
Tel: 65321235/65321236/
65321237
Fax: 65325364

Portugal
2-15-1/2 Diplomatic Building,
Tayuan
Tel: 65323497/65323220/
65323242
Fax: 65324637

Romania
Dong, erjie St., Ritan Rd.,
Jianguomenwai
Tel: 65323442/65323255/
65323879

Russia
4 Beizhongjie St., Dongzhi-
men, Sanlitun
Tel: 65322051/65321381/
65321267
Fax: 5324853

Rwanda
30 Xiushui North St., Jianguomenwai
Tel: 65322193/65321762

Saudi Arabia
1 Beixiaojie St., Sanlitun
Tel: 65324825/65325325

Senegal
1 Ritan Dongyijie St., Jianguomenwai
Tel: 65322593/65322646

Sierra Leone
7 Dongzhimenwai St., Sanlitun
Tel: 65321222/65322174

Singapore
1 Xiushui North St., Jianguomenwai
Tel: 65323926/65323143
Fax: 65322215

Slovakia
Ritan Rd., Jianguomenwai
Tel: 65321531

Slovenia
3-53 Building, Jianguomenwai
Tel: 65326356/65326357

Somalia
2 Sanlitun Rd., Sanlitun
Tel: 65321752

Spain
9 Sanlitun Rd., Sanlitun
Tel: 65321986/65323629/
65323728
Fax: 65323401

Sri Lanka
3 Jianhua Rd., Jianguomenwai
Tel: 65321861/ 65321862
Fax: 65325426

Sweden
3 Dongzhimenwai St.,
Tel: 65323331
Fax: 5323803

Switzerland
3 Dongwujie St., Sanlitun

Tel: 65322736/ 65322737/
65322738
Fax: 65324353

Syria
6 Dongsijie St., Sanlitun
Tel: 65321372/ 65321347

Tanzania
8 Liangmahe South Rd., Sanlitun
Tel: 65322394

Thailand
40 Guanghua Rd.
Tel: 65321903
65321980
Fax: 65325426

Togo
11 Dongzhimenwai St.
Tel: 65322202/ 65322444

Tunisia
1 Sanlitun Dongjie St., Sanlitun
Tel: 65322435/ 65322436

Turkey
9 Dongwujie St., Sanlitun
Tel: 65322650/ 65322347

Uganda
5 Sanlitun Dongjie St., Sanlitun
Tel: 65321708

Ukraine
11 Dongliujie St., Sanlitun
Tel: 65326359/ 65324013/
65324014

The United Arab Emirates
1-9-1 Diplomatic Building,
Tayuan
Tel: 65322112/ 65325083/
65325085

United Kingdom
11 Guanghua Rd., Jian-
guomenwai
Tel: 65321961/ 65321962/
65321963

USA
Embassy
3 Xiushui North St., Jianguomenwai
Tel: 65323831/ 65323431

Consulate
Bruce Building
2 Xiushui East St., Jian-
guomenwai
Tel: 65323431 ext 225

Uruguay
2-7-2 Diplomatic Building,
Tayuan
Tel: 65324445/ 65324413

Venezuela
14 Sanlitun Rd., Sanlitun

Tel: 65321295/ 65322694

Vietnam
32 Guanghua Rd., Jian-
guomenwai
Tel: 65321155/ 65323593/
65325415

Yemen
5 Dongsanjie St., Sanlitun
Tel: 65321558/ 65323394/
65321688

Yugoslavia
1 Dongliujie St., Sanlitun
Tel: 65323516/ 65321693/
65323016

Zaire
6 Dongwujie St., Sanlitun
Tel: 65321995/ 65322713

Zambia
5 Dongsijie St., Sanlitun
Tel: 65321554/ 65321778/
65322058

Zimbabwe
7 Dongsanjie St., Sanlitun
Tel: 65323795/ 65328665/
65323397

图书在版编目（CIP）数据

旅游会话 / 陈蒙惠、殷边编著.
北京：外文出版社，1988.8（2002.5 重印）

ISBN 7-119-00557-X

Ⅰ.旅... Ⅱ.①陈...②殷... Ⅲ.旅游－汉语－口语－对外汉语教学-
教材-汉、英 Ⅳ. H195.4
中国版本图书馆 CIP 数据核字（2002）第 021961 号

责任编辑 曾惠杰

外文出版社网址：
  http://www.flp.com.cn
外文出版社电子信箱：
  info@flp.com.cn
  sales@flp.com.cn

旅游会话

陈蒙惠
殷 边　编著

*

外文出版社
外文出版社出版
（中国北京百万庄大街 24 号）
邮政编码 100037
中国国际图书贸易总公司发行
（中国北京车公庄西路 35 号）
北京邮政信箱第 399 号 邮政编码 100044
1988 年（36 开）第 1 版
2006 年第 1 版第 6 次印刷
（英）
ISBN 7-119-00557-X / H·74(外)
01600(平)
9-CE-2297P